ABOUT THE ROYAL SHAKESPEARE COMPANY

The Royal Shakespeare Company at Stratford-upon-Avon was formed in 1960 and gained its Royal Charter in 1961. This year we celebrate 50 years as a home for Shakespeare's work, the wider classical repertoire and new plays.

The founding Artistic Director, Peter Hall, created an ensemble theatre company of young actors and writers. The Company was led by Hall, Peter Brook and Michel Saint-Denis. The founding principles were threefold: the Company would embrace the freedom and power of Shakespeare's work, train and develop young actors and directors, and crucially, experiment in new ways of making theatre. There was a new spirit amongst this post-war generation and they intended to open up Shakespeare's plays as never before.

The impact of Peter Hall's vision cannot be underplayed. In 1955 he had premiered Samuel Beckett's *Waiting for Godot* in London, and the result was like opening a window during a storm. The tumult of new ideas emerging across Europe in art, theatre and literature came flooding into British theatre. Hall channelled this new excitement into the setting up of the Company in Stratford. Exciting breakthroughs took place in the rehearsal room and the studio day after day. The RSC became known for exhilarating performances of Shakespeare alongside new masterpieces such as *The Homecoming* and *Old Times* by Harold Pinter. It was a combination that thrilled audiences.

Peter Hall's rigour on classical text became legendary, but what is little known is that he applied everything he learned working on Beckett, and later on Harold Pinter, to his work on Shakespeare, and likewise he applied everything he learned from Shakespeare onto modern texts. This close and exacting relationship between writers from different eras became the fuel which powered the creativity of the RSC.

The search for new forms of writing and directing was led by Peter Brook. He pushed writers to experiment. "Just as Picasso set out to capture a larger slice of the truth by painting a face with several eyes and noses, Shakespeare, knowing that man is living his everyday life and at the same time is living intensely in the invisible world of his thoughts and feelings, developed a method through which we can see at one and the same time the look on a man's face and the vibrations of his brain."

A rich and varied range of writers flowed into the company and continue to do so. These include: Edward Albee, Howard Barker, Edward Bond, Howard Brenton, Marina Carr, Caryl Churchill, Martin Crimp, David Edgar, Peter Flannery, David Greig, Tony Harrison, Dennis Kelly, Martin McDonagh, Rona Munro, Anthony Neilson, Harold Pinter, Stephen Poliakoff, Adriano Shaplin, Wole Soyinka, Tom Stoppard, debbie tucker green, Timberlake Wertenbaker and Roy Williams.

The Company today is led by Michael Boyd, who is taking its founding ideals forward. His belief in ensemble theatre-making, internationalism, new work and active approaches to Shakespeare in the classroom has inspired the Company to landmark projects such as *The Complete Works Festival*, *Stand up for Shakespeare* and *The Histories Cycle*. He has overseen the four year transformation of our theatres, he has restored the full range of repertoire and in this birthday year we are proud to invite the world's theatre artists onto our brand new stages.

NEW WORK AT THE RSC

As well as commissioning plays each year from writers we love, we have recently re-launched the RSC Studio to provide the resources for writers, directors and actors to explore and develop new ideas for our stages. We also explore the canon for classics to revive and lost classics to re-discover.

We invite writers to spend time with us in our rehearsal rooms, with our actors and practitioners. Alongside developing their own plays, we invite them to contribute dramaturgically to both our main stage Shakespeare productions and our Young People's Shakespeare.

We believe that our writers help to establish a creative culture within the Company which both inspires new work and creates an ever more urgent sense of enquiry into the classics. The benefits work both ways. With our writers, our actors naturally learn the language of dramaturgical intervention and sharpen their interpretation of roles. Our writers benefit from re-discovering the stagecraft and theatre skills that have been lost over time. They regain the knack of writing roles for leading actors. They become hungry to use classical structures to power up their plays.

Our current International Writer-in-Residence, Tarell Alvin McCraney, has been embedded with the Company for two years. His post was funded by the CAPITAL Centre at the University of Warwick where he taught as part of his residency.

The RSC Literary Department is generously supported by THE DRUE HEINZ TRUST

The RSC is grateful for the significant support of its principal funder, Arts Council England, without which our work would not be possible. Around 50 per cent of the RSC's income is self-generated from Box Office sales, sponsorship, donations, enterprise and partnerships with other organisations.

Supported by
**ARTS COUNCIL
ENGLAND**

JOIN US

Join us from £18 a year.

Join today and make a difference
The Royal Shakespeare Company is an ensemble. We perform all year round in our Stratford-upon-Avon home, as well as having regular seasons in London, and touring extensively within the UK and overseas for international residencies.

With a range of options from £18 to £10,000 per year, there are many ways to engage with the RSC.

Choose a level that suits you and enjoy a closer connection with us whilst also supporting our work on stage.

Find us online
Sign up for regular email updates at **www.rsc.org.uk/signup**

Join today
Annual RSC Full Membership costs just £40 (or £18 for Associate Membership) and provides you with regular updates on RSC news, advance information and priority booking.

Support us
A charitable donation from £100 a year can offer you the benefits of membership, whilst also allowing you the opportunity to deepen your relationship with the Company through special events, backstage tours and exclusive ticket booking services.

The options include Shakespeare's Circle (from £100), Patrons' Circle (Silver: £1,000, Gold: £5,000) and Artists' Circle (£10,000).

For more information visit **www.rsc.org.uk/joinus** or call the RSC Membership Office on 01789 403 440.

[NATIONAL THEATRE OF SCOTLAND]

In 2011, the National Theatre of Scotland celebrates its first five years of creating theatre that excites and entertains audiences at home and beyond, and which makes Scotland proud.

Since our very first productions in 2006, everything we have aspired to challenges the notion of what theatre can achieve. With no building of our own we're free to make theatre wherever we can connect with an audience – a promise we take seriously. Our work has been shown in airports and high-rises, forests and ferries, drill halls and football pitches, pubs and factories.

As Scotland's national theatre, we exist to work collaboratively with the best companies and individuals to produce and tour world class theatre that's for the people, led by great performances, great writers and great stories.

National Theatre of Scotland
Civic House, 26 Civic Street
Glasgow G4 9RH
Scotland
T: +44 (0) 141 221 0970
F: +44 (0) 141 331 0589
E: **info@nationaltheatrescotland.com**

The Scottish Government

The National Theatre of Scotland is core funded by the Scottish Government.

The National Theatre of Scotland, a company limited by guarantee and registered in Scotland (SC234270), is a registered Scottish charity (SC033377).

The National Theatre of Scotland presents
the Royal Shakespeare Company's production of *Dunsinane*
in association with the Royal Lyceum Theatre, Edinburgh.

This production of *Dunsinane*, first performed by the RSC,
was presented by the National Theatre of Scotland at
the Royal Lyceum Theatre, Edinburgh, on 13 May 2011.
The cast was as follows:

SOLDIER	**George Brockbanks**
MALCOLM	**Brian Ferguson**
THE BOY SOLDIER	**Tom Gill**
SCOTTISH SOLDIER/ LORD	**Kevin Guthrie**
SOLDIER/ LORD	**Lewis Hart**
GRUACH'S ATTENDANT/ HEN GIRL	**Lisa Hogg**
SOLDIER	**Joshua Jenkins**
EGHAM	**Alex Mann**
MACDUFF	**Phil McKee**
GRUACH'S ATTENDANT	**Mairi Morrison**
SIWARD	**Jonny Phillips**
GRUACH	**Siobhan Redmond**

All other parts played by members of the Company

Written by	**David Greig**
Directed by	**Roxana Silbert**
Designed by	**Robert Innes Hopkins**
Composition and Sound Designed by	**Nick Powell**
Lighting Designed by	**Chahine Yavroyan**
Movement Director and	
Assistant Director of the Chorus	**Anna Morrissey**
Fights by	**Terry King**
Voice Coach	**Stephen Kemble**
Dramaturg	**Jeanie O'Hare**
Original Casting by	**Helena Palmer CDG**
Additional Casting by	**Anne Henderson**
Archery Consultant	**Ruth Cooper-Brown**

Musicians

Guitar/Mandolin	**Alex Lee**
Percussion	**Ric Chandler**
Cello	**Sarah Willson**

This text may differ slightly from the play as performed

Production Acknowledgments

With thanks to: Heather Marshall, Creative Electric; Neil Packham,
Citizens Theatre Community Company; John MacNeill, Telford College;
Martin Andrews, Weymss & March Estates; the cast who did the
original workshop and the cast and crew from the original production at
Hampstead Theatre, London. Production photographer, Richard Campbell.
Audio description by Mary Plackett and Ridanne Sheridan.
Captioned by Janet Jackson.

THE COMPANY

BRIAN FERGUSON

TOM GILL

GEORGE BROCKBANKS

SOLDIER
trained: George has recently graduated from the Arts Educational School, London.
theatre includes: *Dunsinane* marks his first professional engagement after training. Productions while training include: *Measure for Measure*, *Love and Money*, *Macbeth*, *Present Laughter*, *Golden Boy*, *Antigone*, *The Seagull*, *Someone Who'll Watch Over Me*.
other professional credits include: *Territory* (Lowry/ Pleasance, Islington/ Pleasance, Edinburgh); *A Midsummer Night's Dream* (Shakespeare Youth Festival).

MALCOLM
RSC: *Dunsinane* (original cast, Hampstead, 2010), *Shakespeare in a Suitcase.*
trained: Royal Scottish Academy of Music and Drama.
theatre includes: Previous work for the National Theatre of Scotland includes: *Rupture* (with Traverse, Edinburgh), *Snuff* (with The Arches, Glasgow), *Falling* (with Poorboy). Brian was also a member of the original cast of *Black Watch*, and in 2008-09 he was a National Theatre of Scotland Artistic Associate. Other theatre includes: *Earthquakes in London* (National Theatre); *The Dark Things, Fall* (Traverse); *The Drawer Boy* (Tron).
television includes: *Taggart, Rockface, Still Game, River City, Doctors.*

THE BOY SOLDIER
trained: Tom Gill is a recent graduate of the Guildford School of Acting.
theatre includes: *Territory* (Lowry/ Pleasance, Islington/ Pleasance, Edinburgh); *Spring Awakening* (Ben Kingsley Theatre, Salford). Productions while training include: *Wildest Dreams, This Happy Breed, The Crucible, Measure for Measure, A Trip to Scarborough* (Guildford School of Acting).
film includes: *Eden Lake, The Engagement Party* (short).

DAVID GREIG

WRITER

RSC: *Dunsinane* (original production, Hampstead, 2010), *The American Pilot*.
theatre includes: David is a playwright, screenwriter and director. Previous work for the National Theatre of Scotland includes: *The Strange Undoing of Prudencia Hart*, *Peter Pan*, *The Bacchae*, *Futurology: A Global Review* and *Gobbo*. Other recent theatre work includes: *Midsummer*, *Miniskirts of Kabul*, *Damascus*, *Pyrenees*, *San Diego*, *Outlying Islands* and *The Cosmonaut's Last Message to the Woman He Once Loved in the Former Soviet Union*, *8000m*, *Lament*, *Mainstream*.
translations and adaptations include: *Tintin in Tibet*, *King Ubu*.
radio plays include: *The American Pilot*, *An Ember in the Straw*, *Being Norwegian*.
screenplays and television work include: *M8*, *Nightlife*.
awards include: The Traverse Theatre's 2002 production of *Outlying Islands* won a Scotsman Fringe First, Herald Angel and Best New Play at the Critics Awards for Theatre in Scotland. *San Diego* (Edinburgh International Festival/Tron, Glasgow) won a Herald Angel and the award for Best New Play at the Tron Theatre Awards 2003. David has also won the John Whiting award and a Creative Scotland award.

KEVIN GUTHRIE

SCOTTISH SOLDIER/ LORD

trained: Royal Scottish Academy of Music and Drama.
theatre includes: *Peter Pan* (National Theatre of Scotland/Barbican); *The Glass Menagerie*, *Crime and Punishment*, *Uncle Vanya* (RSAMD); *Mary Queen of Scots got her Head Chopped Off*, *Antigone* (XLC); *Animal Farm*, *Market Boy*, *Dorothy's Wonderful Visit to Oz*, *A Midsummer Night's Dream* (David Lee-Michael); *Adrian Mole* (Basement); *Lords of Creation*, *The Legend of Dragonara*, *Snow White and the Seven Dwarfs*, *Cinderella* (Pace).
television includes: *Fields of Blood*, *Case Histories*, *Adventures of Daniel*, *Half Moon Investigations*, *Still Game*, *The Key*, *Terri McIntyre*.
film includes: *Young Adam*, *Dust* (short), *Penrose* (short), *Brain Damaged* (short).

LEWIS HART

SOLDIER/LORD

trained: Italia Conti Academy, London.
theatre includes: *Life Support* (York Theatre Royal Studio); *Miller* (Etcetera, London); *The Cage* (Pleasance, Edinburgh); *Under Milk Wood* (Space, Edinburgh); *Spotlight Showcase 2010* (Bloomsbury Ballroom).
film includes: *Busking for a Beatdown*, *Ten Glorious Seconds*.

LISA HOGG

GRUACH'S ATTENDANT/HEN GIRL

RSC: *Dunsinane* (original cast, Hampstead, 2010).
theatre includes: *Overtime* (Arcola); *Dallas Sweetman* (Paines Plough); *Scarborough* (Primecut Productions); *Tales of Ballycumber* (Abbey, Dublin); *Loyal Women* (Royal Court); *24 Hour Plays: Begin Again* (Old Vic); *Waning and Waxing, Tarmacking the Belt* (Soho/Theatre Works); *Much Ado About Nothing* (Stafford Festival); *War Crimes Tribunal* (Soho); *Many Loves* (Lilian Bayliss); *Pete and Me* (New End), *In the Jungle of the City* (Drill Hall); *The Wizard of Oz* (Ulster Theatre Co.); *The Fisher King, She Stoops to Conquer, War of Words* (Lyric, Belfast).
television includes: *Waking the Dead, Best: His Mother's Son, Wire in the Blood, Trial and Retribution, The Commander, Fallen, The Royal, Casualty, The Bill, Brookside*.
film includes: *Across the Universe, Almost Adult*.
radio includes: *Dunsinane, Loyal Women*.

ROBERT INNES HOPKINS

DESIGNER

RSC: *Macbeth, A Servant to Two Masters, The Comedy of Errors, The Malcontent* (also West End), *Dunsinane* (original production, Hampstead, 2010).
theatre includes: *Bingo, Wallenstein, Carousel, Goodnight Mr Tom* (Chichester Festival Theatre); *Swallows and Amazons* (Bristol Old Vic); *Wanderlust, Clybourne Park, The Priory, Tusk Tusk, The Pain and the Itch, Redundant* (Royal Court); *Marble* (Abbey); *Dallas Sweetman* (Paines Plough); *Romeo and Juliet, Twelfth Night* (Open Air Theatre, Regent's Park); *The Member of the Wedding* (Young Vic); *Our Country's Good* (Liverpool Playhouse).
opera includes: *Kommilitonen!* (Royal Academy of Music); *Xerxes* (Stockholm); *The Rape of Lucretia* (Snape Maltings); *Billy Budd* (Santa Fe); *Carmen* (Bolshoi); *Lohengrin* (Geneva); *Rigoletto* (Lyric Opera, Chicago); *Betrothal in a Monastery* (Glyndebourne); *Die Soldaten* (Ruhr Triennale/Lincoln Center Festival).
awards include: Opernwelt Set Designer of the Year 2007 for *Die Soldaten*.

JOSHUA JENKINS

SOLDIER

RSC: *Dunsinane* (original cast, Hampstead, 2010).
trained: Royal Scottish Academy of Music and Drama.
theatre includes: *Unrestless* (Old Vic Tunnels); *The World Turned Upside Down* (Òran Mór); *Bed Bug* (Shell Connections). Productions while training include: *Mother Goose, The Ruling Class, Practical Jokers, Innocent as Charged, Macbeth, Much Ado About Nothing* (RSAMD). Joshua also participated in the National Theatre of Scotland's *Diaspora* in 2008.
television includes: *The Fabulous Baker Boys, Doctors, One Night in Emergency, Garrow's Law, Heartbeat, Stopping Distance, Belonging*.
film: *Plots with a View*.

TERRY KING

FIGHT DIRECTOR
RSC: Recent productions include: *Dunsinane* (original production, Hampstead, 2010), *Little Eagles*, *As You Like It*, *The Drunks*, *The Grain Store*, *Hamlet*, *Romeo and Juliet*, *Antony and Cleopatra*, *Morte d'Arthur*, *Othello*, *Hamlet*, *A Midsummer Night's Dream*, *The Histories Cycle*, *Noughts & Crosses*, *Julius Caesar*, *King John*, *Pericles*, *The Indian Boy*, *Merry Wives the Musical*, *Twelfth Night*, *As You Like It*, *Gunpowder Season*.
this season: *Cardenio*, *Macbeth*, *Dunsinane*.
theatre includes: *The Lord of the Rings*, *On an Average Day*, *Ragtime*, *Chitty Chitty Bang Bang* (West End); *Accidental Death of an Anarchist*, *Caligula* (Donmar); *King Lear*, *The Murderers*, *Fool for Love*, *The Duchess of Malfi*, *Henry V*, *Edmund*, *Jerry Springer the Opera* (National Theatre); *Oleanna*, *Search and Destroy*, *Sore Throats* (Royal Court).
opera includes: *Othello* (WNO); *Porgy and Bess* (Glyndebourne); *West Side Story* (York); *Carmen* (ENO).
television includes: *Fell Tiger*, *A Kind of Innocence*, *A Fatal Inversion*, *The Bill*, *EastEnders*, *Measure for Measure*, *Casualty*, *The Widowing of Mrs. Holroyd*, *Death of a Salesman*.

ALEX MANN

EGHAM
RSC: *Dunsinane* (original cast, Hampstead, 2010), *Shakespeare in a Suitcase*.
trained: London Academy of Music and Dramatic Art.
theatre includes: *The Odyssey* (National Theatre, London); *Sunday is the New Saturday* (Edinburgh Festival Fringe); *The Art of Success*, *New England*, *The Permanent Way*, *The Cherry Orchard* (LAMDA).
television includes: *At Home with the Georgians*, *Hustle*.
radio: *Dunsinane*.

PHIL MCKEE

MACDUFF
RSC: *Noughts & Crosses*.
trained: Royal Scottish Academy of Music and Drama.
theatre includes: Previous work for the National Theatre of Scotland: *Mary Stuart*. Other theatre includes: *Pandas*, *Any Given Day* (Traverse); *That Face* (Tron); *Relocated* (Royal Court); *Strawberries in January* (Paines Plough/Traverse); *A Madman Sings to the Moon*, *Julius Caesar* (Royal Lyceum); *Damages* (Bush); *8000M* (Suspect Culture); *Stitching* (Traverse/Bush); *Macbeth* (Landor/Cage); *The Robbers*, *The Boat Plays* (Gate); *Richard III*, *Napoli Milionaria*, *King Lear* (National Theatre); *Lady Betty* (Cheek by Jowl).
television includes: *Garrow's Law*, *Ghost Squad*, *The Family*, *Band of Brothers*, *Crime Traveller*, *Heartbeat*, *Silent Witness*, *The Bill*, *Taggart*, *Soldier, Soldier*, *The Place of the Dead*, *Lost in France*, *Lovejoy*.

film includes: *The Shepherd, George and the Dragon, Beginner's Luck, Simon Magus, Joan of Arc, Simon Magus, The Debt Collector, The Star, The Lost Battalion, Clash of the Titans.*

ANNA MORRISSEY

MOVEMENT DIRECTOR AND ASSISTANT DIRECTOR OF THE CHORUS

RSC includes: *Dunsinane* (original production, Hampstead, 2010), *Antony and Cleopatra, The Grain Store, The Drunks, The Tragedy of Thomas Hobbes, I'll Be the Devil, The Cordelia Dream, Timon of Athens.*
trained: Lewisham College and the Central School of Speech and Drama.
theatre includes: Previous work for the National Theatre of Scotland: *Caledonia* (with the Edinburgh International Festival). Other movement direction and assistant direction credits include *Bus Stop* (New Vic); *My Dad's a Birdman* (Young Vic); *The Comedy of Errors* (Royal Exchange); *Hansel and Gretel* (Opera North); *Hanover Square* (Finborough); *101 Dalmatians* (Northampton Theatre Royal); *The Barber of*

Seville, Manon Lescaut (Opera Holland Park); *Dr Faustus* (Resolution! The Place); *Restoration* (Headlong); *Mother Courage* (English Touring Theatre); *The Tempest, A Warwickshire Testimony, As You Like It, Macbeth* (Bridge House); *The Taming of the Shrew* (Creation); *Richard III* (Cambridge Arts); *Hamlet* (Clifford's Tower, York); *The Arab-Israeli Cookbook* (Tricycle); *Human Rites* (Southwark Playhouse); *Julius Caesar* (Menier Chocolate Factory); *Tamburlaine the Great* (Rose, London).
Anna made her directorial debut with *Beating Heart Cadaver* at the Finborough Theatre in April 2011.

MAIRI MORRISON

GRUACH'S ATTENDANT

RSC: *Dunsinane* (original cast, Hampstead, 2010).
trained: Royal Scottish Academy of Music and Drama.
theatre includes: Previous work for the National Theatre of Scotland: *A Dead Man's Dying* (with Òran Mór). Other theatre includes: *Jacobite Country, The Seer* (Dogstar); *Eat Your Heart Out* (Òran Mór); *Roghainn nan Daoine/The People's Choice, Metagama* (Theatre Hebrides); *Raining Rubbish* (Motherwell Theatre); and her self-penned solo show *Beasts of Holm* (Edinburgh Festival Fringe).
film and television includes: *Taggart, Na Bonnachain, Bad Brown Owl, PC Alasdair Stewart, Gruth is Uachdar, Lostbost, Broadford or Bust, Na Daoine Beaga, Ioma Rud, Baile Mhuilinn, Falach Fead, Miughlaigh, An Roghainn.*
radio: *Seven Deadly Sins.*

JONNY PHILLIPS

SIWARD

RSC: *Dunsinane* (original cast, Hampstead, 2010).
trained: Royal Academy of Dramatic Arts, London.
theatre includes: *True Love Lies* (Royal Exchange); *Othello* (Cheek by Jowl/world tour); *In the Solitude of Cotton Fields* (Almeida); *The Grace of Mary Traverse, Gone, Who Knew Mackenzie* (Royal Court); *The Way of the World* (Lyric, Hammersmith); *Hedda Gabler* (Donmar/tour); *Sugar Sugar* (Bush); *Three Sisters* (Whitehall); *Design for Living, Mother Courage and Her Children, Anna Karenina, Celestina, Mary Stuart, No Man's Land, Death of a Salesman, Friends and Lovers* (Citizens, Glasgow).
television includes: *Dark Matters, I Shouldn't Be Alive, Forgotten Few, Spooks, Holby City, Hustle, 10 Days to War, The Bill, Belle de Jour, Warriors: Attila the Hun, Heartbeat.*

film includes: *You Instead, Soft, The Things We Leave Behind, Dreamland, Bronson, The Edge of Love, Vanity Fair, The Last Great Wilderness, Beautiful People, Titanic, The Last of England, Prick up your Ears.*

NICK POWELL

COMPOSER AND SOUND DESIGNER

RSC: *Dunsinane* (original production, Hampstead, 2010), *The Grain Store, The Drunks, God in Ruins.*
theatre includes: Previous work for the National Theatre of Scotland includes: *Realism* (with Edinburgh International Festival), *The Wonderful World of Dissocia* (with EIF/ Tron, Glasgow/ Drum, Plymouth), *Futurology: A Global Review* (with Suspect Culture); *The Wolves in the Walls* (with Improbable). Other theatre includes: *Get Santa, The Priory, Relocated, The Vertical Hour* (Royal Court); *The Crucible* (Open Air Theatre, Regent's Park); *Falstaff* (Centro Dramático Nacional, Madrid); *Penumbra, Tito Andronico* (Animalario, Madrid); *Urtain, Marat-Sade* (Animalario/ CDN, Spain); *Paradise* (Ruhr Triennale Festival); *Panic* (Improbable); *The Family Reunion* (Donmar).

television and film includes: *Beneath the Veil, Death in Gaza, Lip Service* and the Spanish feature *Dispongo de Barcos*. He has also scored three of the films of visual artist Phil Collins.
other work includes: Nick has toured and recorded with many bands including McAlmont & Butler, Strangelove, and Astrid. He is one half of OSKAR, who have performed live scores for three Prada fashion shows in Milan, exhibited installations at the V&A, London and the CCA, Glasgow.

SIOBHAN REDMOND

GRUACH

RSC: *Dunsinane* (original cast, Hampstead, 2010), *The Comedy of Errors, The Spanish Tragedy, Much Ado About Nothing, Twelfth Night.*
trained: Bristol Old Vic Theatre School.
theatre includes: Previous work for the National Theatre of Scotland includes: *The House of Bernarda Alba, Mary Stuart*

Other theatre includes: *The Secret Garden* (Festival Theatre, Edinburgh); *Dido, Queen of Carthage* (National Theatre, London); *A Midsummer Night's Dream* (Shakespeare's Globe); *The Lunatic Queen* (Riverside Studios); *US and Them* (Hampstead); *The Prime of Miss Jean Brodie, As You Like It* (Royal Lyceum); *Les Liaisons Dangereuses* (PW Productions); *Perfect Days, Shadowing the Conqueror* (Traverse, Edinburgh); *An Experienced Woman Gives Advice* (Royal Exchange, Manchester); *The Trick is to Keep Breathing* (Tron, Glasgow/Royal Court London).

television includes: *Mind Away, Boy Meets Girl, The Bill, Lift, The Catherine Tate Show, Eastenders, New Tricks, The Smoking Room, Sea of Souls, Ed Stone is Dead, Holby City, Every Woman Knows a Secret, In the Red, Wokenwell, The High Life.*

film includes: *Beautiful People, Karmic Mothers, Captives, Duet for One, Latin for a Dark Room.*

radio includes: seven series of *McLevy* for Radio 4.

ROXANA SILBERT

DIRECTOR

RSC: *Dunsinane* (original production, Hampstead, 2010), Associate Director. *A Tender Thing, Brixton Stories.*

this season: *Little Eagles, Dunsinane.*

Roxana was previously Artistic Director of Paines Plough (2005-2009), Literary Director at Traverse Theatre (2001-2004), Associate Director at Royal Court (1999-2001) and Trainee Associate Director at West Yorkshire Playhouse (1998-1999).

theatre includes: *Orphans, Roaring Trade* (Paines Plough); *Being Norwegian, Between Wolf and Dog* (Paines Plough/Òran Mór); *Long Time Dead* (Paines Plough/Plymouth Theatre Royal/Traverse); *Strawberries in January* (Paines Plough/Traverse); *Under the Black Flag* (Shakespeare's Globe); *After the End* (Paines Plough/Traverse/Bush/59e59 /international tour); *Dallas Sweetman* (Canterbury Cathedral); *Whistle in the Dark* (Citizens Theatre); *Precious, Blond Bombshells* (West Yorkshire Playhouse); *Property* (National Theatre Studio); *Damages* (Bush); *The Slab Boys, Still Life* (Traverse/national tour); *The People Next Door* (Traverse/Theatre Royal, Stratford East); *Iron* (Traverse/Royal Court); *15 Seconds, Greenfields* (Traverse); *The Price* (Bolton Octagon); *Top Girls, Translations* (New Vic, Stoke); *Cadillac Ranch* (Soho); *At the Table, Still Nothing, I Was So Lucky, Been So Long, Fairgame,*

Bazaar, Sweetheart (Royal Court); *Mules* (Royal Court/Clean Break Theatre Co./national tour); *Slash Hatch on the E* (Donmar).

radio includes: *Hysteria, Billiards, Japanese Gothic Tales, The Tall One, The Tape Recorded Highlights of a Humble Bee, The Good Father, Brace Position.*

CHAHINE YAVROYAN

LIGHTING DESIGNER

RSC: *Dunsinane* (original production, Hampstead, 2010), *God in Ruins.*

this season: *Little Eagles, Dunsinane.*

theatre includes: Previous work for the National Theatre of Scotland includes: *Caledonia, Realism* (with Edinburgh International Festival), *The Wonderful World of Dissocia* (with EIF/Tron/Drum, Plymouth), *Elizabeth Gordon Quinn.* Other theatre includes: *The Death of Klinghoffer* (Scottish Opera/EIF); *The Cosmonaut's Last Message to the Woman He Once Loved in the Former Soviet Union* (Tron); *San Diego* (Tron/EIF); *Fall, Damascus, Outlying Islands, 15", Iron, The Speculator, Gagarin Way, Anna Weiss, King of the Fields, Knives in Hens, Perfect Days, The Architect* (Traverse); *Gilt, Dumbstruck* (Dundee Rep); *Jane Eyre* (Perth); *Scorched* (Old Vic Tunnels); *Get Santa, Wig Out!, Relocated* (Royal

Court); *Medea/Medea*
(Gate); *Il castigo sin
venganza, Fuenteovejuna*
(Madrid); *The Lady from the
Sea, The Comedy of Errors,
Three Sisters* (Royal
Exchange); *Il Tempo del
Postino* (Manchester
International Festival);
Orphans, Dallas Sweetman
(Paines Plough).
other work includes: Site-
specific projects include:
*Light Touch, Dedicated,
Focal Point* (Scarabeus);
Salisbury Proverbs (Station
House Opera); *Dreamwork*
(at St Pancras Chambers);
Spa (at the Elizabeth Garrett
Anderson Hospital); *Deep
End* (at Marshall St. Baths)
and the New Year's Eve
celebrations for the City of
Bologna, Italy.
Chahine has also lit fashion
shows for Givenchy,
Clemens Ribeiro, Hussein
Chalayan and Ghost.

TECHNICAL TEAM

Naomi Pirie (Royal Lyceum Theatre)
Company Stage Manager

Heather Wilson
Deputy Stage Manager

Gabriel Bartlett
Assistant Stage Manager

Raymond Short
Props Technician

Tony King
Stage Supervisor

Neill Pollard
Lighting Supervisor

Claire Carroll
Sound Supervisor

Marion Harrison
Wardrobe Mistress

Elayne Dexter
Wardrobe Assistant

Helena Rose
Wigs & Make-up Technician

Sarah Marshall (Royal Lyceum Theatre)
Production Carpenter

David Greig

Dunsinane

ff

faber and faber

First published in 2010
by Faber and Faber Limited
74–77 Great Russell Street, London WC1B 3DA

Typeset by Country Setting, Kingsdown, Kent CT14 8ES
Printed and bound by CPI Group (UK) Ltd, Croydon, CR0 4YY

A CIP record for this book
is available from the British Library

ISBN 978–0–571–26021–8

4 6 8 1 0 9 7 5

Acknowledgements

I would like to thank the following people
who participated in workshops in Pitlochry 2008
and Edinburgh 2009. Their work was invaluable
in creating the shape of this play:

David Ireland, Tom McGovern, Ferdy Roberts,
Danny Sapani, Samantha Young, Ramin Gray,
Jennifer Black, Craig Conway, Brian Ferguson,
Kieran Hill, Antony Strachan and Stephen Wight.

I would also like to thank Dr Fiona Watson,
Jeanie O'Hare and Roxana Silbert for their help
in preparing the script for production.

David Greig, February 2010

Characters

Siward
an English general

Osborn
his son

Macduff
his Scottish lieutenant

Egham
his English lieutenant

The Sergeant

The English Army

Gruach
the Queen

Gruach's Women

A Scottish Soldier

A Scottish Boy

Malcolm
the King of Scotland

McAlpin
Moray
Kintyre
Luss
Clan Chiefs of Scotland

The Boy Soldier
The Hen Girl
Boy Prisoners

DUNSINANE

'What wood is this before us?'
Shakespeare, *Macbeth*

Lines spoken by soldiers and archers
of the English army are prefixed
by a long dash —

[Dialogue in square brackets is spoken in Gaelic.]

One

Dawn.

Rain.

The English army prepares for battle.

We boarded our ships at the Thames mouth.
There were two thousand of us and also
Some horses for the knights to ride and animals
For us to slaughter on the way.

We stood on the Essex shore a mess of shingle,
Some of us new and eager for a fight and others
Not so sure but all of us both knowing and not knowing
What lay ahead of us.

Scotland.

Scotland. Where we would install a king.

I have not been on a boat before,
Not a boat like that before, not on a boat like that
On a sea like that, swells rising about us,
Waves clashing and retreating about us,
A day and a night and a day of it feeling sick
And every single moment of it afraid
But excited too – in the hull with my companions
Talking against the sea with stories,
And one or two had a song or two
And one man showed me how to fight
With a spoon for a sword – laughing –
Laughing at me – me acting the goat –
And all of us both knowing and not knowing what lay
Ahead of us.

War.
And that some of us would die in it.

In time the fleet found the softer waters
Of the river Forth and we landed in a place called Fife –
Which is a wild place compared to Kent –
And there we camped in woods near the abbey of Inchcolm.
And waited until at last he came to us – Siward
Our commander – and he told the sergeants it was time
To prepare us for the fight.

Sergeant You –

— Sir?

Sergeant Be a tree.

— Yes, Sir.

Sergeant You and you and you – make yourself
undergrowth –

— Yes, Sir.

Sergeant Come on!
You're supposed to be a forest!
You – make the noise of a bird –

— Sir?

Sergeant What?

— Is this all right, Sir?

Sergeant What's that?
Come on, think.
What's a forest got?

— Sir?

Sergeant What's its stuff?

— Trees?

Sergeant Trees yes trees and apart from trees?

— I don't know.

Sergeant Close your eyes –
   Conjure up a wood – walk in it – look about you –
what do you see?

— The wind.

Sergeant What else?
   What do you see – look hard – what do you see now?

— Badgers.

Sergeant Badgers yes and what else?

— . . .
— . . .
— . . .
— Nothing, Sir.

Sergeant Exactly – nothing.
   Good.
   Nothing.
   What does nothing look like?

— Nothing.

Sergeant No. Nothing looks like something – what?

— Darkness.

Sergeant That's it – good lad.

The forest's made of trees and in between the trees the
darkness. It's not the something of it that fools the eyes
but the nothing in between. All of you – get on your
knees, dig your hands into the bog water – smear your
faces with black mud – we'll make a forest of you yet –
come on!

   Preparations continue.

— Lord Siward's coming, Sir.

Sergeant Stand ready.

The boys become a forest.
  Siward enters with Osborn, his son, beside him, and
Macduff.

Sergeant Lord Siward, Macduff, Lord Osborn.
May I present –
Birnam Wood.

A forest, birds sing, trees move in the breeze, shadows.
Siward and his son walk through the forest.

Siward Look, Osborn.

A forest of English yew, each branch of which can bend
and twist but when it is knotted together in a thicket – it
is impenetrable – a sword cuts one branch and another
springs up to take its place.

Here –

Take a branch.

Put mud on your face,

Take my sword.

If these boys are old enough to fight then so are you.

Siward gives Osborn his sword.

Tomorrow before the sun's up we'll surround the tyrant.
He'll wipe the sleep from his eyes and find himself not in
his bed in his castle but deep in the middle of the wild
wood with an English spear at his throat.

The sun sets.

Siward raises his sword.

Siward To Dunsinane!

Siward Dunsinane and the fight to take it!

*

The English army advances through the night to
Dunsinane
   Rain, mist and darkness.
   Sentries are killed.
   The English overwhelm the castle.

*

A room in the castle.
   A bed.

A Scottish Soldier fires arrows from a vantage point onto
the battle outside.
   He speaks to someone whom we cannot see; he speaks
in Gaelic.

Scottish Soldier [This is your last chance.
   Go now.]

   Gruach and the Boy emerge from the shadows.
      Gruach kisses the Boy.

[Go now.
   Run. Run.]

   The Boy runs out of the room.
      Gruach looks at the battle out of the window.
      The battle is near now.

   The Scottish Soldier runs out of arrows.

[It's too late.
   They've taken the door.]

   Outside the door they hear the shouts of the English
   Soldiers.

[Hide yourself.]

Gruach [No.]

Scottish Soldier [They'll kill you.]

English voices outside.

— Clear.

— Clear.

— Clear.

Gruach hides herself.

— This door's barred.

— Hold on.

— Stand back.

The Scottish Soldier prepares himself for the assault.
He holds a knife.

English Soldiers break down the door.
They are bloody from the fight.

A moment of looking between them.

The Scottish Soldier attacks the Soldiers.

The Soldiers subdue the Scottish Soldier and knock him to the floor.

A Soldier holds him.

— He cut my leg.
Fuck.
Ayah.

A Soldier cuts the Scottish Soldier's throat.
The Scottish Soldier dies.

— Clear.

— Clear.

— Clear.

The Soldiers – having established clarity – rest.

One looks out of a window.

— He was firing from here.
  He could see right over the courtyard.
  He could just pick a target.
  Look at them.
  There must be twelve men dead down out there.

— He'd have got more if he hadn't run out of arrows.

— He ran out of arrows?

— Look.

— Why did he fight?
  Why didn't he just surrender?

— He knew we'd kill him either way.

They examine the dead man's bow.

— It's small.

— I had one like this when I was a kid.

— He had a good eye.

— Check the hall.

Soldiers exit to check other parts of the castle.

The room is empty apart from the body of the man.

From off:

— Clear!

— Safe!

— All clear!

Gruach emerges from the shadows.
  She makes for the door.
  She hears a man outside groaning, clanking with armour.

She returns to her hiding place.

Egham enters.
He has an arrow in his arm.
It hurts.

He sees the dead Scottish Soldier.

Egham Scottish bastard.

He kicks him.

Ow.
Scottish fucking bastard.
Ah ah ah ah.

Egham sits on the bed.

Lads!
. . .
Lads!
. . .
Lads!

Egham tries to stand.
Egham slumps.

A moment.

The other Soldiers return.

— This tower's safe.

— What now?

— There's still fighting.

— We've done our share.

— Rest.

Egham groans.

— Christ.

— Who's that?

— Egham.

— Egham?

— Lord Egham of Egham.

— Is he one of ours?

— Yes.

— Is he dead?

— He's breathing.

— Let's see.

Egham Ahhhhhhhhh!

— He doesn't look well.

— Sir.

— Sir.

— Sir.

Egham Lads –

— Sir.

Egham It's my arm.
The pain is very bad.

— Give him a drink and we'll pull the arrow out.

Egham No! No!

— Sir, it's best if we pull it out.

Egham I want the surgeon.

— The longer it's in, Sir, the longer it's sore.

Egham I will wait for the surgeon.

— All right, Sir – only – there's a few hundred boys lying dying on the field out there – arms and legs and all sorts cut. It might be a while before the surgeon comes.

Egham I'm tired.
I feel tired beyond words.
Wake me when the surgeon comes.

Egham slumps again.

— What shall we do with him?

— He looks very pale.

— Leave him.

The Soldiers sit.

— What's happening out there?

— Looks like things are coming to an end.

— Shouldn't we go out there and help?

— We've done enough.

— Enough?

— Look out there.
The field's covered in dead.
It'll all be over soon.
No sense any more of us dying now.
The castle's taken.

— Have we won?

— Looks like it.

— Whoo!
We won!
We fucking won!
First fight I've ever been in.
Whooo!

— You did well.

— Did I?

— You did.

— Where's Siward?
  Where's our flag?

— He's out there – on the hill.

— What's he doing?

— Fighting.

— But we've won.

— Still have to fight.

One Soldier has a found a silver goblet.

— Look at this. Seen this?

— Put that back.

— What?
  , There's more in there.
  Look!

— Leave it.

— Why?

— All the treasure gets gathered in one place and once
the fighting's over it gets divided.

— I know, but no one needs to know.

— No.

— Are you worried about him?
  He's asleep.

— I said no.

— No one can see.

— When the fighting's over there'll be a dividing of the treasure and we'll get our share. In the meantime count yourself lucky. We're alive. Let's enjoy it while we can.

The Soldiers relax.

— Did anybody notice any women?

— There were some in the kitchens.

— Alive?

— Dead.

— Oh.

— There's bound to be some alive ones somewhere.

— There'll be women.

— I know but it would be good if there was one here now.

— Well, there isn't.

Egham groans.

— I wish he wouldn't make that noise.

— It's annoying.

— He has got an arrow in his arm.

— Everybody's had an arrow in their arm.

— I haven't.

— You will.

— What's it like?

— Not as bad as he's making out.

— It sounds sore.

— Could be worse.

— Could it?

— Could be dead.

— Have you been in a lot of battles?

— A few.

— What was this one like? Compared to other battles you've been in?

— Good.

— Why was it good?

— I didn't get hurt.

— Right.
  It's my first battle.

— You hurt?

— No.

— Good.

— I thought it went by really quick.

  . . .

  There was a bit when I was crossing the bridge and I was slashing away in front of me and – I wasn't even looking – I just –

He demonstrates.

And there was two or three of them moving back away from us but one came forwards and I didn't even mean to but I cut down hard onto his shoulder and my sword went straight through – I must have hit here and the sword went just – shhhush – and took his arm right off. I didn't even mean it and his arm just came away. He screamed.

— It's just leather they wear.

— Is it?

— Just leather for armour. Only some have metal.

— Is leather worse than metal?

— Depends.

— On what?

— You're alive.
  Does it matter?

— I'm interested.

— Leather's worse than metal if you're in a fight with a man with a broadsword.

— When's it better?

— When you're trying to run through a forest.

Siward enters.

The Soldiers stand to attention.

Siward Stand easy.

The Soldiers rise.

Is this the last tower?

— Yes, Sir.

Siward Did you clear it?

— It's clear, Sir.

Siward Who's this?

Siward looks at the prone Egham.

Siward Egham! Get off your back. The work's not finished yet. There are Scots lords running in the forest. Up! Up!

Egham groans.

Siward What's wrong with him?

Egham My arm.

— Arrow, Sir.

Siward You – bring me some beer.

Egham Siward.
   I've been wounded.

Siward I can see.

Egham I just feel so unbelievably tired.

Siward You'll be fine.

Egham I was telling the lads.

— Ale, Sir.

Siward Here, drink this.

Egham Thank you.

Siward That's it, drink it down.

Egham So cold.

Siward Take this blanket.

Egham Will the surgeon come soon?

Siward Soon, yes.

Egham Good.

> *A signal from Siward.*
>   *Soldiers hold Egham.*
>   *Siward cuts around the arrow.*
>   *He rips the arrow from Egham's arm.*
>   *Egham screams.*

Egham You bastard!

Siward More pain now, less pain later.

Egham whimpers.

You – you – you – take him down to the kitchens and burn out the wound.

Soldiers take Egham away.

Siward You – boy – stay.
Keep an eye on the courtyard.

Boy Soldier Yes, Sir.

The Boy Soldier looks out of the window.

Siward takes off some armour.
  He rests on the bed.

Siward What do you see?

Boy Soldier Smoke. A lot of smoke.

Siward We set light to the forest. Drove them out and into the hills. Eventually they'll find their way back to their homes and their farms. We'll set a new king in Dunsinane and then summer will come and then a harvest and by next spring it'll be as if there never was a fight here.

You'll be amazed how quickly a battle can disappear.

Macduff enters.

Boy Soldier Stand back, Sir!

Macduff Hey!

Macduff easily subdues the boy.

Siward Too quick, boy. Well done for your good intentions but here's a lesson for you in war, always learn the face of your general.

Macduff.

Macduff releases the boy.

Siward Good to see you.

Macduff Siward.

Siward What's your report?

Macduff The tyrant is dead.

Siward Good.

Macduff He was running when we caught him.
A spear in his back.
They brought him to me on the hill above the wood.
He couldn't speak but I looked into his eyes and there was still life there.
It was a pleasure to extinguish it.
I cut his throat.
His head's on a stick in the castle yard.

Siward It's over.

Macduff Yes.

A moment.

Siward Is there something else?

Macduff Osborn.

Your son.

He was with the Cumbrians.
They were riding in pursuit through the forest.
Osborn was riding at the front. He was with the leaders moving through the woods. As they got near one of the Scots lords turned suddenly and shot a bolt.

It must have been a lucky shot.

Through the trees like that.
Shooting as they ran.
Luck.

Siward Osborn is dead.

Macduff I'm sorry.

Siward Where's the wound?

Macduff On the chest.

Siward Can it be a mistake?

Macduff No.

Siward Thank you.
  You can go.
  Go.

  Macduff exits.
    A moment.

Boy Soldier Sir . . . do you want me to go as well?

Siward No. Stay.

  The Boy Soldier sits next to Siward.
    The Boy Soldier observes, perhaps attempts to
  comfort Siward.
    Siward holds the boy.

  Gruach leaves her hiding place.

  She stands in front of Siward, in plain view.

  The Boy Soldier sees her.

Boy Soldier Hey.

  The Boy Soldier grabs her.
    Siward draws his sword.

Gruach Get off me!

Boy Soldier She bit me!

Siward She's fighting because you hold her.
  . . .
  Let her go.

26

The Boy Soldier lets go of her.

She stands.

Siward Woman, your castle has fallen.

. . .
Do you understand?

. . .
I am Siward.
I am England.

Do you speak English?

Gruach Yes.

Siward What is your name?

Gruach Gruach.

Siward Gruach.
Gruach, what work do you do here in Dunsinane?

Gruach Work?

Siward What is your place here?

Gruach My place here is Queen.

*

The Great Hall in Dunsinane.
Malcolm on the throne.

Siward You told me she was dead.

Malcolm Did I?

Siward You told me she went mad and died.

Malcolm Mmm.

Siward You told me the tyrant had lost the support of
the chiefs and he had no son and his queen had died of
madness and so there would be no resistance to you but on

the other hand we were likely to see a swift and general acceptance of your rule and the chance to establish a new and peaceful order.

That's what you said.

Malcolm Yes.

Siward Well – she's not dead.

Malcolm So it would seem.

Siward Not even sick.

Malcolm No.

Siward You lied to me.

Malcolm Siward – there's a small thing I ought to say if you don't mind – and I'm not trying to avoid your general point, but there's an important clarification I must make before we go any further. In Scotland to call me a liar is really unacceptable – if – here in the great hall for example – a man were to call me a liar that would – essentially – demand a violent response – a statement like that being – as it would be – a matter of honour – and so usually the way we manage this sort of thing in Scotland is by being careful not only not to tell lies – but also to be very very careful about the way we hear and understand words. So for example – if a person in Scotland says 'It seems a person has died' we tend to hear that word 'seems' – 'seems' – and of course that word makes a difference. Isn't that infuriating? It's silly and of course it means that every discussion is fraught and people have to pussyfoot around when obviously one simply wants to cut through the nonsense and describe the facts of the world as they are – but there it is – that's how things are – and so – before we go any further – I suppose what I'm asking you – Siward is – really – and this is just for clarification – are you calling me a liar?

Siward No.

Malcolm Well, that's a relief.

Siward I understood that the Queen was dead.

Malcolm It turns out that was a mistaken understanding.

Siward It would seem so.

Malcolm Mmm.

. . .

Of course the whole thing would be easier if she were dead.

Siward What?

Malcolm Well, as long as she's alive she will tend to be a focus for dissent.

Siward I thought you said the chiefs were simply waiting for you to arrive and establish yourself before they would pledge their allegiance and crown you king.

Malcolm Siward – do you mind if I ask – are you going to continue with this insistent literalness? 'You said' – 'He said' – you sound like a child.

Siward I'm sorry.

It seems I was mistaken in my understanding about the Queen.

I was also – apparently – mistaken in my understanding about dissent.

Is there anything else in Scotland about which my understanding may have been mistaken?

Malcolm I know. I know. It's quite ridiculous isn't it? I'm King of this country and even I don't understand it. Sometimes I think you could be born in this country. Live in it all your life. Study it. Travel the length and breadth of it. And still – if someone asked you – to describe it – all you'd be able to say about it without fear of contradiction is – 'It's cold.'

29

Siward Is there anything else about the current situation in Scotland about which my understanding may have been mistaken?

Malcolm One thing.

Siward What?

Malcolm She has a son.

> *Macduff draws a map of Scotland.*
> *He shows Siward the political lie of the land.*

Macduff There are many clans and families but there are two parties that sit at the heart of everything in Scotland – Alba in the west and Moray in the north.

Siward Malcolm is Alba –

Macduff Malcolm is McAlpin which is the first royal line of the Alba.

Siward And the tyrant was Moray?

Macduff No.
    The Queen is from Moray.
    The tyrant was from Mull.

Siward Sorry, I'm lost.

Macduff Over here. Mull is small and usually fights on the same side as Argyll, which is Moray, but historically Mull's past belongs to Alba – by cousinship.

Siward What does that mean?

Macduff It means the tyrant came from nowhere.
    His power belonged to the Queen. The Queen is the eldest princess of Moray. It's she who holds the allegiance of the clan and it's her power that she's keeping for her son.

Siward The tyrant was a usurper. He was from nowhere. He stole the throne by murder. Surely the son of a usurper has no legitimate claim.

Macduff Yes – except the tyrant's son isn't the tyrant's son.

Siward What?

Macduff The tyrant's son belongs to the Queen's first husband. Her father married her first to a prince of Alba with the aim of unifying Scotland under one crown. Gruach bore that prince a son – the rightful heir. But then the tyrant came from Mull and murdered the boy's father.

The tyrant married Gruach and he became king.

He adopted the boy as his own.

The boy is the rightful heir.

Siward How strong are the party of Moray now?

Macduff They have strongholds here and here. In Rannoch and the glens they are with Moray – to the south in Glen Lyon the people are allied with Alba – they're kin to McAlpin there but not friends of his – there's been murders between them and so on. To the east lies Angus where there's good land but no fortune and seemingly no wisdom either, so Angus usually wait until they see which way power slides before adding their weight to whichever seems to be the winning side –

Siward We are the winning side.

Macduff For now.

Macduff Here – Strathspey is mine – I have two sisters married there – Sutherland is with Moray. Here in Fife – these are my lands as well – but here and here are here – surrounding me – are all branches of the tree of Moray.

Siward So we have here – here and here all with the Queen.

Macduff Yes.

Siward And the rest with Malcolm.

Macduff It's not as simple as that.

Siward Why?

Macduff Not everyone who is against the Queen is with Malcolm.

Siward Malcolm is the new king. He can create a stable kingship here based on peace and general acceptance of law – and eventually he will unite Moray and Alba and Mull and Angus and whoever and whatever and wherever. Malcolm will make a new situation where everybody works together in pursuit of the kingdom's common interest.

Macduff To create that situation would require a very large army and it would take a very long time.

Siward Is there another choice?

Macduff Kill the Queen.
Put her head on a stick in the castle yard.
End it.

*

Gruach sits with the body of the old king.
Gruach's women sing a lament.
Siward watches.

Gruach He was a good king.
He ruled for fifteen years.
Before him there were kings and kings and kings but not one of them could rule more than a year or so at most before he would be killed by some chief or other.
But my king lasted fifteen years.
My king was strong.

Siward Your king murdered your first husband.

Gruach Yes.

Siward You don't seem to mind.

Gruach I asked him to do it.

Siward Did he always do the things you asked?

Gruach Mostly.

Siward Where is your son?

Gruach I don't know.

Siward Is he hidden here?

Gruach No.

Siward You know I will search.

Gruach He escaped. He's out in the hills now. I don't know where.

Siward Is he alive?

Gruach Yes.

Siward How do you know?

Gruach If he were dead – word would have come to me.

Siward But you have no proof.

Gruach He's alive.

Siward Gruach, I have no quarrel with you. I came here to install Malcolm as king so as to secure England's northern border. My job is to build a new kingdom – not to settle old grudges. So I have to clear away the past now. I have to uproot now and clear away all past claims and –

    That way there is a chance that we can establish a fair peace in Scotland in which every clan can flourish – including yours.

New government can't be built on top of old wounds.

Gruach What do you want from me?

Siward I want you to renounce your son's claim to the throne.

Gruach My son doesn't *claim*.
   My son *is* the King.
   It's not a matter about which he has a choice.
   My son is my son.
   My son is the son of his father.
   My son's father is dead.
   My son is the King.

Siward What would you do – if you were me?

Gruach If I were you I would not be here. If I were you I would be at home guarding my own land. Not fighting on behalf of some other man's land. A man too weak and corrupt to hold his own land himself.

Siward It's in England's interest to have peace in Scotland.

Gruach We had peace.
   Until you came along.

   Go home.

   Don't waste any more of your English lives here.

   Go home before you're driven home.

Siward Gruach, I'm not asking you for a favour. I'm giving you a chance. Your son is wandering in those hills like a beggar. If you swear alliegance to Malcolm he could be given more titles, more land. He could be given the bishopric of Argyll. He could be safe. You could be safe. Scotland could be be at peace.

Gruach The moon could rise at daytime and we could call it night.
   The sun could rise at night time and we could call it day.
   My son would still be king.

Siward Is the grieving finished?

Gruach Yes.

Siward My men will take your husband's body to Iona.
They will bury him there.

Gruach Our custom is that I go with him on the boat
beside him.

Siward That's not possible.

Gruach I should go with him.

Siward No.

The grieving is finished.

*

The castle courtyard.
*Soldiers bring bodies into the castle yard and lay them
out in rows.*

— Leicester.
Leicester.
Dunno.
Essex.
Cumbria.
Newcastle.
York.
York.
York.

— I don't think this one belongs to us.

— Let's have a look.

— No – he's not ours.

— Kent?

— How do you know he's not ours?

— The belt.

— It looks the same as mine. He looks pretty much the same as me.

— How many more are there?

— Another couple of fields' worth.

— Bring another load.

The cart is taken out to be refilled with bodies from the field.
  The soldiers rest.

Siward and Macduff enter.

— Sir.

Siward Where is Osborn?

— There, Sir.

— We put him specially there.

Siward walks among the rows of bodies.
  He finds the body of his son.

Siward My son.

I should have stayed with him.

Macduff He's with you now.

Siward Thank you.

Macduff Siward.

Osborn died in a good cause.

But the cause is unfinished.

Let me settle the matter of the tyrant's queen.

Malcolm can't do it. If Malcolm killed her that would be an act which would have to be revenged. Let me do it.

And then we'll find the son. He's being hidden somewhere in the near vicinity. We'll soon catch him.

Siward And kill him too?

Macduff Let them take revenge on me.

Siward No.

There's been too much blood spilled already.
Boy!

— Yes, Sir.

Take my son away. Bury him with the others. Mark the place with a stone so I can find it later.

— Yes, Sir.

Siward Moray, Alba.

Macduff –

None of this – stuff – matters.

What matters now is sense. What matters now is justice.

*

The great hall.
Malcom on the throne.
Siward enters.

Malcolm Is she dead?

Siward No.

Malcolm Oh.

Siward Why would you think she were dead?

Malcolm I just thought she might have fallen ill.

Siward She's well.

Malcolm Good.

Siward She's under my protection.

Malcolm What do you propose to do with her?

Siward I don't propose to do anything.

. . .

I propose to let you decide what to do.

Malcolm Is that wise?

Siward When I say you – I mean Scotland.

You are Scotland.

Macduff and I will visit every clan chief in the country – we will go to each one of them and listen to them. We'll find out what they want and then, when we have understood, we'll invite them here to talk.

Malcolm Talk.

Siward We'll invite them to a parliament here in Dunsinane. We'll find a consensus. Let Scotland decide the fate of her queen. And then, and only then, we'll crown you king.

Unchallenged.

Siward prepares for a journey.

Siward Egham!

Egham Yes, Sir.

Siward Find billets for the men. Make an inventory of the castle's treasure. Find the cattle.

Make Dunsinane a garrison.

Tell the men we'll be in Scotland a little longer than we expected.

Two

SUMMER

The English army establish themselves in Dunsinane.

All through summer – or what they call summer –
Siward had us marching over land – or what they
Call land – from house to house – to eat food –
Or what they call food – with the chiefs of every clan.

From clan to clan we'd march day on day
And in every place we'd get sharp glances
And we'd smile back – you know – for the children,
Offer out our hands to them with nuts or something
But always the children leaving our hands alone and
Then always one child hiding behind some woman
And the woman's eyes burning at us.

And you'd want something burning here anyway
    because, mother,
I don't know if you've ever heard this but Scotland is cold!
You've not felt coldness until you've felt the coldness
Of the air here and the beds and the nights,
And so you'd want a burning of eyes or anything
Just to warm yourself on those long marches
When you'd think in this next village surely there'll be
A fire – a hearth we can stand against – but no –
Every time just cold damp air and the eyes of women.

And we began to wonder what sort of country this is
Where everything that in England was normal –
Summer, land, beer, a house, a bed – for example –
In Scotland – that thing would turn out to be made of
    water –
This is what you learn here – nothing is solid.

You look at the ground ahead of you and you guess
And you make a jump and suddenly you're up to your
    waist in mud,
You think this forest floor can take your weight,
You think over there's a lake,
But one's mud and the other's rock.
And whichever way you walk you hurt yourself.
So you can tell this, mother, to any boys you happen
    to meet,
If they say they're being sent up north to join us –
Say to them this one thing – tell them – my son says,
    in Scotland
Always be careful where you put your feet.

*

*The hall is full of all the valuable objects of the castle.
    Soldiers bring more into the hall in chests.*

Egham I hate this country.
    One set of wooden plates.

Boy Soldier One set of wooden plates.

Egham God never meant people to live this far north,
you know.
    One tapestry showing a woodland scene.

Boy Soldier One tapestry showing a woodland scene.

Egham I know we're not supposed to attempt to deduce
God's intentions, but just a glance tells you – if God had
meant people to live this far north he would have given
us fur.
    Four barrels of – some type of beer.

Boy Soldier Four barrels of beer.

Egham Of course the Scots *are* hairy.
    One Bible.

Boy Soldier One Bible.

Egham But that alone can't explain it.
  They must marshal some other kind of heat inside
them.
  Four silver goblets.

Boy Soldier Four silver goblets.

Egham Grudge.
  That's what it is.
  An assortment of alder cups.

Boy Soldier An assortment of alder cups.

Egham Their grudge keeps them warm.
  Even when it's so cold my balls are shrunk tight
against my bum. Their dislike of us is keeping those
bastards warm.
  That's the maddening thing.
  They hate us and all we do is make the hairy
ungrateful treacherous bastards more comfortable.
  Seven blankets which smell of dogs.

Boy Soldier Seven blankets which smell of dogs.

Egham I'm not even supposed to be here you know.
  Some dogs.

Boy Soldier Some dogs.

Egham Some horses.

Boy Soldier Some horses.

Egham I'm supposed to be a monk.
  Four beds.

Boy Soldier Four beds.

Egham I'm supposed to be a monk giving myself over to
God on some island somewhere.
  Two dozen sacks of flour.

Boy Soldier Two dozen sacks of flour.

Egham Peace and quiet and cloisters.
Food from the abbey garden.
Ten skins full of wine.

Boy Soldier Ten skins of wine.

Egham Wine from the abbey vineyard.
Women.
One silver candlestick.

Boy Soldier One silver candlestick.

Egham I was supposed to be a monk
But my father insisted – fight –
There's a war in Scotland – go and win us some land and a manor house.
Fifteen sacks of barley.

Boy Soldier Fifteen sacks of barley.

Egham Eighteen sacks of oats.

Boy Soldier Eighteen sacks of oats.

Egham What is the point?
What is the fucking point?
I ask you.
Boy?

Boy Soldier Sir?

Egham I ask you?

Boy Soldier What do you ask me, Sir?

Egham What's the point in being alive?

Boy Soldier I don't know, Sir.

Egham The point of life is to survive – you just have to try to get through as much of life alive as you possibly can and use whatever time you've got and whatever methods you can muster to make the journey as comfortable as is possible.

Stay alive and be comfortable.

Those are the purposes of life.

And they're also the two things that are hardest to do when you spend your summer fighting a fucking war in Scotland.

Siward Egham.

Egham Siward. You're back.

Siward Complaining again, Egham?

Egham No, Sir. Just – taking stock.

Siward Boy – go outside and guard the door.

The Boy Soldier exits.

How's the inventory?

Egham Working through it, Sir.

Siward What's the value so far?

Egham Five chests full of Scottish coins.
Six gold candle holders.
Twelve silver cups. Twelve silver plates.

Siward Only twelve?

Egham Yes, Sir.

Siward Maybe they eat off wood.

Egham Or else they've hidden the rest.

Siward What about the animals?

Egham Horses, dogs.
Cows, sheep, geese, hens.

Siward How many?

Egham I don't know. Some.

Siward How many exactly – how many geese? How many sheep? How many hens?

Egham A normal amount.

Siward Numbers, Egham.

Egham You want me to count livestock?

Siward We must count everything, Egham.
  We'll not steal.

Egham The army has to eat.

Siward We have to eat and so do the Scots.

Egham The men need to be paid and –

Siward We'll pay the men and we'll feed them, but the Scots need a treasury.

Egham Right.
  I mean normally, Sir, there is a dividing and –

The men won't last long on food and water and no excitement.

Siward The Scots think that we're here to subdue them. It's our job to prove them wrong. We'll take no women and no gold and we'll take not one beast more than we need. We will make them to trust us. Understand?

Egham Yes, Sir.

Siward Good.
  How's your shoulder?

Egham Sore.

Siward You'll be back fighting soon.

Egham I don't think so, Sir, it really is sore.

Siward It's a small wound got in a good cause.
Wear the scar proudly, Egham.
Some lost more.

Trouble from off.
  The Boy Soldier enters.

Boy Soldier Sir – sorry – she won't – I can't –
Wait.
Will you just wait.
Jesus.
Sorry.

Gruach enters.

Siward Gruach.

Gruach I am not comfortable.

Siward I'm sorry to hear that.

Gruach I want my clothes. I want my bed. And I want
my women.

Siward I have only just returned from travelling, Gruach.
If it's about your living arrangements I'm sure Egham will
help you.

Gruach I'm sure he won't.

Siward What exactly is the problem?

Gruach I want my clothes.

Siward I will arrange for some clothes to be brought to
you.

Gruach I don't want 'some' clothes I want my clothes.
My clothes have been taken.

Siward What do you mean – 'taken'?

Gruach Two chests full of my clothes are missing from
my rooms.

Siward And you think they were taken?

Gruach They didn't walk.

Siward Who took them?

Gruach Your men took them.

Siward What would my men want with your clothes?

Gruach A queen's clothes.

Siward What would my men want with a queen's clothes?

Gruach I don't know. What would your men want with a queen's clothes?

Siward I'm sorry to hear of your troubles. Go back to your rooms and I'll have some men look for the missing items.

Gruach They won't have to look far. That chest you're sitting on. That chest contains my clothes.

Siward looks at Egham.

Egham Blankets and curtains.

Siward This chest contains blankets and curtains.

Gruach It contains my wardrobe.

. . .
Open it.

They open the chest.
   It contains the Queen's clothing.

Gruach Did you intend to wear them?

Siward What's this?

Gruach Is that the English habit?

Egham I remember now.

46

One of the lads – brought it down – looks similar to – other – similar chests – I'll have a lad take it back up.

Siward Is there anything else missing?

Gruach A cup.

Siward Is it an important cup?

Gruach My father gave it to me when I was born.
It has the emblems of my family engraved on it.
Three snakes devouring a moon.

Siward Do we have the cup?

Egham It's not on the inventory, Sir.

Siward We'll try to find it.

Gruach And I want my bed.

Siward You have a bed.

Gruach I want *my* bed. I want to occupy *my* rooms – not the room at the back of the tower where you've put me – And I want my women.

Siward And if you had your clothes and this cup and your rooms and your women and your bed – would you be comfortable?

Gruach Yes.

Egham Sir – Malcolm insisted she be kept in the rooms at the back.

Siward Move her.
She may no longer be queen.
But she is still a woman – and this is still her house and we're her guests in it.
See to it, Egham.

Egham Yes, Sir.

Siward You – boy – go with her and be her guard.

Boy Soldier Yes, Sir.

Gruach exits with The Boy Soldier.

*

The Great Hall.
Soldiers bring treasure.
Malcolm looks at the goods.

Malcolm Is this mine?

Siward It belongs to the treasury.

Malcolm My treasury.

Siward Scotland's treasury.

Malcolm Mine.
I am still Scotland.
Aren't I?

Siward I hope so.

Malcolm How was your trip?

Siward Good.

Malcolm How are our chiefs?

Siward They have their grievances.

Malcolm No surprises there.

Siward There are plenty of disputes to be unravelled. But if we persevere I believe that we can make a picture of the world which everyone agrees true.

Malcolm Make a picture of betrayal. They'd all agree on that.

Siward Malcolm, your position is strong. The Queen doesn't have the support she might think. Some of the Moray chiefs talk about compromise.

Malcolm Don't trust a word they say. They're flies in her web. Nothing is spoken in Scotland without her knowing about it.

Siward If she's speaking her wishes through them then let's take her at her word.

Malcolm I wondered if she might eat something.

Siward What?

Malcolm A sick eel.

A bad hen.

Some glass.

Siward It's in our interest to keep Gruach alive and comfortable.

Malcolm I notice you moved her room.

Siward She said she was not comfortable.

Malcolm Spider.

Siward That's ridiculous.

Malcolm Is it?

Siward She's the only person in Scotland with the power to settle this quarrel.

A settled quarrel will make for a settled kingdom.

Malcolm A settled kingdom is a kingdom in which everyone is dead.

Siward That's not how it is in England.

Malcolm Lovely England.

I would have liked to have stayed in England. I like the way people speak in England. I liked hunting in those broad oak woods. I liked the dogs there and the horses.

I liked the way that nobody in England wanted to kill me.

There's very little pleasure for me in being Scotland.

Give me back England and let someone else have my money.

Siward It's not your money.

Malcolm I saw smoke.

Siward Smoke?

Malcolm Yesterday, coming from Dunkeld.
Was there an incident?
Any news of the boy?

Siward No. One of our patrols found two of the tyrant's lieutenants hiding in a barn in the village. They had weapons and seemed to be preparing for an ambush. We burned the barn. They're dead.

Malcolm What about the farmer?

Siward What farmer?

Malcolm The man whose barn it was.

Siward He's safe.

Malcolm Good.

. . .
Is he one of mine?

Siward I don't know.

Malcolm Mmm.

Only – if he's one of mine he probably ought to have sacrificed himself for me when the tyrant's men came – oughtn't he? Rather than hiding them in his barn.

Siward They probably threatened him. He probably had no choice.

Malcolm Yes.

Still.

If you're one of mine . . . that carries with it certain obligations.

Siward He's an old man.

Malcolm Mine have to be seen to defend me.

The appearance of that is quite important.

If one of mine fails to defend me and I don't punish him then I appear weak.

Siward You appear merciful.

Malcolm Mmm.

Siward At any rate, burning his barn should be punishment enough.

Malcolm You must think us a very quarrelsome lot. Us Scots.

Siward The English quarrel too.

Malcolm Siward – I was raised in England – in those lovely oak woods where everything is sun-dappled and the forests are full of wild boar and deer and the tables always full of beer and ham – but here we are rock, bog, forest and loch. I am tied to mine. If one of mine doesn't defend me to the death – well – and as it happens I hate this aspect of things – but there it is – that man has to die.

Siward What if this man was not one of yours? What if he came from another clan?

Malcolm Then there would be no problem.

If he's of another clan we'd expect him to hide his own. It might be good in that situation to appear merciful.

. . .

Is he from another clan?

Siward He is a farmer, who is alive, with a family who will now be able to work for you and serve you and pay taxes and –

Malcolm Is he mine?

Siward I will not kill a man for doing a reasonable thing.

Malcolm Of course.

Of course. You're right.

I'm sorry, Siward, you have to forgive me, sometimes I forget. The thinking in this country is so full of traps, you have to walk around in such circular paths, sometimes I forget that another type of thinking even exists.

Straight.

Do what you think is right.

I'll do everything in my power to help you.

Siward exits.

Malcolm talks with some of his men.

Malcolm Donald.

Donald Sire.

Malcolm Send out two men. Find this man. Kill him and his family and divide his possessions amongst the villagers.

Malcolm's men take weapons and leave.

*

Gruach's women prepare the Queen's new rooms. Egham enters.

Egham Excuse me, My Lady.

Gruach Egham. What do you want?

Egham I just wanted to check that you were comfortable now.

Gruach For the time being.

Egham Do you have everything you need – clothes – things?

Gruach Yes.

Egham The cup you mentioned.
   The silver cup.
   I found it.

Egham shows her the silver cup.

Gruach Where was it?

Egham I took it.

I took your clothes.

Not to wear but to give to my soldiers to take back to their wives and daughters.

I took these things because we won.

You understand.

Siward wants peace.

But I want money.

I just want you to know where I stand.

Gruach Thank you.

Egham I want you to see that I will be honest with you.

Gruach You will be honest with me – about the fact that you are dishonest.

Egham If we both know where we stand. Perhaps we can help each other.

I know you don't want us to be here.

Some of us don't want to be here either.

Nonetheless we are here and so – we ought to make arrangements – so as to make our stay as comfortable as possible.

Egham gives her the silver cup.

Gruach Does Siward know you're here?

Egham No.

The problem with Siward is that he's a good man. Good men are very difficult to negotiate with.

Gruach You are not a good man.

Egham No.

Gruach What do you want?

Egham I want safe passage to market for my men to buy and sell goods.

I want my convoys unmolested.

Gruach What do you offer me in return?

Egham What do you want?

Gruach Would you betray your own side?

Egham It depends what you mean by 'betray'.

Gruach Malcolm's men are looking for my son.

I want him taken to safety with my people in Glen Lyon.

Egham Wouldn't you prefer a Scottish guard for your boy?

Gruach I couldn't trust anyone.

It's better that he's with an English patrol. Your men have no reason to betray him and Malcolm would have no reason to suspect. Take him to safety and my people will leave you to trade unmolested.

54

Egham Where is he?

Gruach One of my people will take you to him.

Egham How will I recognise him?

Gruach He has the mark of my family on him.

Three snakes devouring a moon.

She gives him back the cup.

Gruach For you.

Take it to market.

You'll get a good price for it.

Consider it a gesture of goodwill.

*

Evening in the castle yard.
The English army butcher cattle.

— Butcher said he'd finally found the castle herd up somewhere in the forest.

— Oh –

— They'd hid them out of the way while the fighting was happening.

— Fair enough.

— But the herdboy had been killed in the battle so no one knew where the cows were. You'd think they'd keep the herdboy with the herd, wouldn't you?

— Yeah.

— But according to butcher it was more of a case of them going – we need everybody out there fighting – you, boy, here's a spear   and then next thing you know one of our arrows get the herdboy – and then it's a case of dead women all over the kitchen and eventually our butcher comes in and he finds someone who's still got a tongue in her head and he says – RIGHT, BITCH, WHERE'S THE CATTLE! – and whoever it is, this half-alive one – she doesn't know – and then butcher's angry – COURSE YOU FUCKING KNOW, LEAD ME – and this half-alive one – whoever he is – she don't speak English and everything's all jumbled up anyway so – there's pointing and there's shouting and anyway – so it takes a week before butcher finally finds the cattle, and the point is – all that time the cows were just wandering happily in the forest getting fat – funny.

— Not that funny.

— What happened to the half-alive woman?

— I don't know.

. . .

. . .

— I'm not going to tell you stories any more.

— Why not?

— You are not a good audience.

— Grumpy.

— Hungry.

— I really want a fuck.

— We're not exactly starving.

— Not if you count eating shit.

— It's not shit – that's not right – it's just weird.

— Horse food.

— Oats.

— Cow tonight, though. You can't go wrong with cow.

— I don't know.

— Pretty much just roast the thing.
What can go wrong with that?

— There'll be something. It won't be cow, it'll be Scottish
cow and it'll taste of shitty water. There's bound to be
something. Or it'll have bits in it.

— Scottish oats.

— There's too much bits of stone in them.

— Something will be wrong with it.

Commotion.
A wounded soldier is brought into the courtyard by
some comrades.

— What happened?

— We were patrolling.

— In the woods down near the river.

— They came at us.

— A lot of them.

— They were waiting.

— They got Tom.

— Put him down.

— Where?

— Anywhere –

— Don't put him down in the blood.

— He's all blood, it doesn't matter.

— Awww God, I feel sick.

— Let's see.

— It's his leg.

— Let's see.

— Might be something we can do.

— He's breathing.

— Look.

— What?

— Look at this.

— Ohhh.

— Never saw that.

— His chest's cut right open.

— Is he breathing?

— He's still breathing.

— Ohh shit.

— What should we do?

— Poor Tom.

The wounded man screams.

— MOTHER!

Silence.

— Kill him.

— What?

— Do it.

— DO IT!

They kill the wounded man.

— What you staring at?
Clean this up.
Clean this up and get back to butchering.

The Soldiers clear away the body.

— This country.

— Stones and shitty water and the food's shit.

— You wonder why we're here.

— You wonder why we want the place.

— You wonder why they give a fuck.

*

In Gruach's rooms the women prepare a drink over a cauldron.
As they work, they sing.
The Boy Soldier watches.

Boy Soldier Is it true that you eat babies?

Gruach Babies?

Boy Soldier They say you eat babies.

Gruach They say the Scots eat babies?

Boy Soldier Oh – no – I mean –

Gruach What do you mean?

Boy Soldier I was asking if it's true that *you* eat babies?

Gruach Me?

Boy Soldier Yes.

Gruach They say that?

Boy Soldier They say that your husband would –

Gruach Would what?

Boy Soldier They said he'd murder people and when he'd murdered them, he'd . . .

Gruach Yes?

Boy Soldier Subdue their wives and –

And that when there was a baby –

Gruach What?

Boy Soldier They say he'd give it to you – and you would eat it.

Gruach They say that?

Boy Soldier Yes.

Gruach What they say –

Boy Soldier Yes.

Gruach It's true.

Boy Soldier Jesus.

Gruach Have you never eaten baby meat?

Boy Soldier Me – no.

Gruach Don't you eat baby meat in England?

Boy Soldier No – not in Kent, anyway.

Gruach You should try it.

Boy Soldier I don't think so.

Gruach It's delicious.

Very tender.

Boy Soldier That's nice singing.

They do nice singing, don't they?
Your ladies.
Lovely.
What is it?

. . .

What's the song?

Gruach It's not a song.

Boy Soldier What is it?

Gruach It's a curse.

Boy Soldier On who?

Gruach You.

Boy Soldier Oh.

Gruach Drink it and you'll turn into a bird.

Boy Soldier Right.

Gruach Fly away home.

*Gruach offers a cup of the hot drink to the Boy
Soldier.*

What's the matter?

Don't you want to go home?

Siward enters.

Siward Gruach.

Gruach Siward?

Siward Out.

Gruach What?

Siward There is a boy dead.

Out – out of these rooms – now.

Boy – get her out.

Gruach Boy – wait!

What's going on?

Siward There is a boy dead.

Out there – in the dust of the castle yard. In amongst the cattle offal and the mud.

A boy. Dead.

He was killed by men who wore your colours.

Gruach Mine?

Siward You knew.

Gruach What did I know?

Siward You directed them to our patrol.

Gruach How?

Siward, I'm a prisoner here. How could I possibly have any idea about what goes on out there in the forest?

Siward You asked me to move your room.

Gruach Because I wanted to return to my own bed, yes.

Siward From this window you can see every time the gate is opened and every time a patrol leaves and you can see the direction in which they ride.

Gruach I have better things to do with my time than spy on your men.

Siward You saw them leave and then you sent a signal.

Gruach How?

Siward I don't know – Light from a mirror. The words of a song. The clothes you wear at the window.

In this country anything can contain a message.

Gruach Siward –

Why would I do this?

I'm under your protection.

At this moment you are the only thing standing between me and death at the hands of one of Malcolm's assassins. It would be insane for me to behave in a way which would lead you to distrust me.

There is a war in this country but it's a war between Malcolm and me.

I have no interest in England.

Siward Someone dressed in your colours killed one of my boys.

Gruach Credit me with a queen's wit, Siward. If I wanted an English boy killed – and I don't, but if I did – don't you think I'd have my women add to their signalling song the instruction – 'Do it – and when you do it – do it dressed in Malcolm's colours'?

Of course you're angry, Siward, you're entitled to be angry, you've been deceived.

But not by me.

Ask yourself this: who benefits from your anger at me? Who would want you to be so angry with me that you might want to kill me? Who?

Siward There is a boy dead.

Gruach I know.

I know.

Siward's anger is gone. The threat is gone.

Siward I was sent here to restore peace and I am trying to do that job as reasonably as I can.

Gruach I know.

Siward And out there is a boy dead.

Each boy who dies, I feel it.

Each boy who dies on whatever side, I feel it.

Gruach I know.

Siward Do you?

Gruach I do.

A moment.

Siward I'm sorry.

I shouldn't have disturbed you.

Please . . . forgive the intrusion.

Siward goes to leave.

Gruach Siward.

Stay.

Talk.

Siward No – it's best if I go.

Gruach Why?

You've talked with all the rest of Scotland. Talk with me.

The women have heated some wine.

Drink.

Gruach takes some up with a ladle.
Pours it into a cup.
She offers it to Siward.

Boy Soldier Sir!

Siward What?

Boy Soldier Sir – that drink is a curse.
It'll turn you into a bird.

Siward What are you talking about?

Boy Soldier She told me.

Gruach It's a magic potion.
I eat babies.

She drinks the wine.

Gruach Mmm.
Blood.

She offers the drink to Siward.

Siward Boy, go.

Find Egham. Tell him to take a patrol down into the
village and find out what anyone saw of the ambush.
Tell him to report to me later.

Go.

The Boy Soldier leaves.
Siward takes the drink.

Siward What type of bird?

Gruach What do you think?

Siward I think a falcon.

Gruach I think a cuckoo.

Making your home in another bird's nest.

Siward drinks.

He checks he hasn't turned into a bird.

Siward Still here.

Gruach For now.

Sit.

I'm bored of being a witch. I'm bored of queens and commanders. I'm bored of being stuck in this room. Siward, I have no company worth the name left with me in Dunsinane. You're a guest in my rooms. Let's pretend for a moment that we're not enemies but only what we appear to be. A man and a woman drinking wine.

And talking.

No more than that.

Siward sits on the bed.
Gruach sits beside him.

Gruach Is something wrong?

Siward No.

Gruach Is there something you want?

Siward No.

Gruach What?

Siward The bed.

The tapestries.

The women.

It's not what I'm used to.

Gruach You're the Lord of Northumberland. You must know comfort in your own castle.

Siward My castle's empty.

Gruach Don't you have a woman there?

Siward No.

Gruach You're like my husband.

Siward Am I?

66

Gruach He was a soldier.

He liked tents and fires and fields.

He didn't like courts or kings.

Siward But you do.

Gruach I like being Queen.

Why do you smile?

Siward You're honest.

Gruach Did you expect otherwise?

Siward No.

Gruach Give me your hand.

Siward Why?

Gruach Let me read your palms.

Siward Why?

Gruach You're occupying my country.

I want to see your future.

Siward hesistates.

Siward These documents are state secrets.

Show me yours first.

Gruach I have nothing to hide.

She offers her hands.

What do you see?

Siward I don't know.

Whatever it is, it's written in a language that I can't read.

Gruach Try.

67

Siward White.

Snow.

Gruach Now me.

Siward offers her his hands.

She takes them.

Siward What?

Gruach Fighting.

Siward What else?

Gruach Nothing else.

A moment.

Siward Your touch is gentle.

Gruach Does that surprise you?

Siward No.

Gruach Had you imagined my touch?

Siward Yes.

Gruach You imagined my touch and now here I am touching you.

Siward Maybe we should be careful.

Gruach Why?

Siward What would your people say if they saw you now?

Perched on the hand of England like a tame bird.

Gruach What type of bird?

Siward A falcon.

Gruach Falcons are never tame.

They just choose their allegiances very carefully.

Siward Gruach,

Did your men kill my soldier?

Gruach No.

Siward Did you give them orders?

Gruach My men know what I want without me having to form it into words.

Siward What do you want now?

Gruach I think you know.

Siward goes to kiss her.

She lets him.

They kiss.

They withdraw.

Gruach Is this usually how you treat your enemies?

Siward I've never met an enemy like you before.

Gruach Like me?

Siward Captivating.

Gruach Captive.

Siward Both.

Gruach Ahh!

You're an elegant talker, Siward, I'll give you that, but for me –
To seduce a man in English – it's like dancing wearing wooden shoes.

Siward Were you seducing me?

Gruach It seems so.

They kiss again.

Again they withdraw.

Gruach We don't need to be enemies, Siward. You said yourself there is no quarrel between us. Malcolm is a weak and venal man. He's no king. Why can't England's ally in Scotland be me? Put your power together with mine.

Siward How?

Gruach You have no woman, Siward.

You have no home.

Marry me.

Siward Maybe you really are a witch.

Gruach I am not a witch but I am the Queen of Scotland.
    And if you marry me.
    You can be king.

Siward Is that possible?

Gruach Do you feel my breath now on your hand?

Siward Yes.

Gruach We are alive.
    Everything is possible.
    Everything.

> *Gruach kisses Siward.*
> *He kisses her back.*
> *The women close the curtains of the bed.*
> *The women sing.*

*

Two Archers fire arrows at a tapestry.

— I'm going to hit that woman right in the tit.

— In the tit, you reckon?

— I reckon.

— All right.

— Dear God, please make it that if I hit that woman in the tit then . . . then make it that I'll touch a tit tonight.

One Archer fires.
The other Archer looks.

— Right in the tit.
Thank you, God.

— Whose tit?

— What do you mean, whose tit?

— Whose tit are you looking to touch tonight? Are you interested in any old tit or in some particular tit?

— I'm not following you, Edward.

— For example. God could easily say: well, here's a tick to bite you on your own tit tonight, Tom, and then you'd have a scratch of your hairy scroffy tit and think bloody tick and God would say – well, there you go, Tom, that's you with a tit touched – that's me fulfilled my side of the bargain.

— I think not.

— I think so.

— I think God has more – has deeper – has higher things in mind than – I think God knows what I mean when I ask for a touch of a tit – I think.

— It's a bold thing to ask a question of God. He's not going to make it easy for you.

— I don't think he's out to trick me.

— No?

— No.

— He's let you end up here.
In this arsehole of a country.

— Still.
I think he understands that if I must be stuck in this arsehole of a country it's reasonable enough for me to ask him to mitigate things a bit with a little tit touch.

— Tits tits tits.

— What?

— All this talk? Have you got some – is there a woman lurking?

— No.

— A woman in your head there?

— Well.

— Who?

— The hen girl.

— Sweet merciful Jesus.

— I know.

— It all makes sense to me now. So . . . what you're asking God is – will he let you get a hand on the hen girl tonight.

— And he's just said yes.

— But has he? Look – we'll seek clarification. The huntsman's cock. I'm going to take aim at the huntsman's cock. Dear God – if I hit the huntsman's cock then that means Tom gets to touch the hen girl's tit, if I miss then that means it'll be some other person's tit he touches – for example, his own.

— All right.

The second Archer fires.

— Thigh.

— Bollocks.

— Sorry.

— That's quite a disappointment.

— Still – hold on though – there's no reason to think it might not be another good-looking woman's tit you get a hold of –

— I suppose so.

— And – also – there's nothing in what God's telling us to say you won't get a touch of the hen girl's arse.

— I know, but –

— The events of tonight contain as many possibilities as there are stars.

— Still.
I had my eye on her tits all week.

— My go for a wish now. What should I aim for?

— The kid's face.

— The kid's face. All right.

— Right in the mouth.

— Dear God, please make it that if I hit the kid's face right in the mouth then . . .

— What?

— Then make it that I get to touch the hen girl's tit.

— You bastard.

The second Archer fires. He hits the kid's mouth.

— God's sending us a very clear message, my friend.

— Your go.

The first Archer raises his bow.

— What's your target?

— Christ's hat.

— What are you asking for?

— Justice.

The Archer points.
Egham enters.
The arrow points directly at Egham.

Egham Jesus!

— Sorry, Sir.

Egham You could have – you should have – issued a warning call.

— Sorry.

Egham A clear shout.

— Sorry.

Egham It's just arrows. I don't like – after my –

— Sorry, Sir.

Egham Here – here's the money from last time. I've got another job for you.

— Sir?

Egham Gather four men and find the girl who looks after the hens. She'll take you to her uncle. Walk with her through the forest. She knows the way. When you get there the uncle will give you a Scottish boy to look after.

You'll know him because he'll have a tattoo – three snakes and a moon. Accompany the boy and the old man to the head of Glen Lyon. Leave them at the yew tree in Fortingall.

Be back by tomorrow and let no one know of the trip.

As usual.

— Yes.
 The hen girl?

Egham Yes.

— Could I do that job? I would like to do that job.

Egham No – I've got a different job for you.

— What?

Egham Manure. Gather the manure from the stables, put it onto a cart. Sell it for whatever you can get.

Egham and the second Archer leave.

— Manure?
 Bollocks.

I want justice.

The first Archer fires. He misses.

Bollocks, God!
 What happened to justice!

*

Morning.
 Siward and Gruach in bed together.

Gruach's women, nearby the bed, are preparing food.

Siward What are they saying?

75

Gruach They're just talking.

Siward What about?

Gruach Breakfast.

Siward I don't like to be in the presence of people talking secretly.

Gruach You could learn our language.

Siward Your language is hard to learn.

Gruach We like it that way.

Siward Why?

Gruach Your English is a woodworker's tool.
Siward.
Hello, goodbye, that tree is green,
Simple matters.
A soldier's language sent out to capture the world in words.
Always trying to describe.
Throw words at the tree and eventually you'll force me to see the tree just as you see it.
We long since gave up believing in descriptions.
Our language is the forest.

Siward Teach me.

Gruach speaks.

Gruach [Maybe you already speak our language.
Do you?]

Siward What did you say?

Gruach I asked you if you understood what I was saying.

Siward How do you say 'yes'?

Gruach [No.]

Siward [No.]

Gruach Yes.

Siward Ask me again.

Gruach [Maybe you already speak our language.
  Do you?]

Siward [No.]

  Gruach's women laugh.

Your women are laughing at me.

Gruach I'm sorry.

Siward Look at you smiling. You smiling and your women
laughing at me. Which of us is really the conqueror here
and which of us the conquered?

Gruach Oh, you're the conqueror.

Siward Am I?

Gruach You invaded my country.

With your powerful army.

You took it.

Laid waste my land.

Burned.

Raped.

And now I'm your prisoner.

To do with as you will.

  Gruach and her women laugh.

Siward You're mocking me.

Gruach Trust my laughter if you hear it, Siward.
  I only laugh with men I like.

Siward What if I don't hear laughter?

Gruach I'm laughing behind your back.

Siward The chiefs are arriving for the parliament.
We have to be ready.

Gruach They can wait.

Siward I have to go.

Gruach I. Have. To. Go.
Your words thump like a fat man on stilts.
There is a dance of leaving – Siward.
Try to learn the steps.

Siward Look at you.

Beautiful bird.

You have your claws in my wrist.

Gruach Take off my ties then. and let me find my quarry.

They kiss.

Siward Now I must cast you off.

*Siward leaves the bed.
He gets dressed.*

*

*The clan chiefs of Scotland and their entourages arrive
in Dunsinane for the gathering. Gifts are exchanged.
Protocols observed.*

Macduff That's Ross – he's wearing the Moray colours –
that's a sign because the Morays have distrusted him for
a long time. See how he embraces Golspie? Golspie's with
Moray too. Look at that – kisses – easy laughter.

Siward They're friends.

Macduff They don't trust each other.

Siward What?

Macduff If they trusted each other they wouldn't need to demonstrate it.

Siward You know this?

Macduff Yes.

Siward Then – but – if it can so easily be seen then –

Macduff It's a demonstration for your benefit, not mine. Now look there – this is Macneill. He's come from the islands. See the way he stands apart. They've been sent on behalf of Macleod and the Lordship of the Isles.

Siward I should introduce myself.

Macduff No.

Siward But he's an ambassador.

Macduff They sent Macneill as a messenger in fact because everyone knows that the Coll – Macleod's brother – is staying with his wife's family nearby in Stirling. It's Coll who should be here but Macleod's sent Macneill. It's a snub.

Siward A snub to whom?

Macduff You. The Isles are demonstrating their primary allegiance is to Norway, not to England. They want you to know how unimportant you are. That's their message.

Siward But I didn't – I don't understand the message.

Macduff It's not important that the message arrives, what matters is that it's been sent.

Siward When do I speak?

Macduff I'll call you at the end.

Siward Who speaks first?

Macduff Malcolm.

> *The parliament has gathered.*
> *Gruach enters.*
> *All eyes on her.*
> *She sits.*

> *Malcolm rises.*

Malcolm Look at you.

Dull.

Every time I try to become excited by the prospect of ruling this country the truth comes sidling in to put out whatever flames of passion my patriotic sentiments might have managed to kindle and my heart feels cold again. You're all thieves. Thieves and the sons of thieves. Mothered by whores. I don't mean anything insulting by saying this – unless the truth is insulting.

It's a country of your making. I've just come back to it.

If you make me king I promise you one thing only – total honesty. In that spirit I offer you the following. I will govern entirely in the interests of me. In so far as I give consideration to you it will be to calibrate exactly how much I can take from you before you decide to attempt violence against me. I will periodically and arbitrarily commit acts of violence against some or other of you – in order that I can maintain a more general order in the country. I will not dispose my mind to the improvement of the country or to the conditions of its ordinary people. I will not improve trade. I will maintain an army only in order to submit you to my will. As far as foreign powers are concerned I will submit to any humiliation in order to keep the friendship of England.

There are some positives.

I like dancing.

So I imagine I will hold big dances.

I like music and singing so when I visit you in your several castles you can look forward to having a good time for many days in a row.

And, most important of all, you need not waste even a minute of your long cold nights wondering about whether you are in or out of my favour. You are out of my favour. Now and always.

Macduff We thank Malcolm for speaking. He's spoken clearly and he's been heard. Now I invite McAlpin of Alba to speak on behalf of his people.

Siward He's not made himself popular.

Macduff It's fine.
 Most of the chiefs don't speak English.
 The ones that do know he's joking.

Siward Why would he joke about his own kingship?

Macduff So we understand he's telling the truth.

Siward What is it – a joke or the truth?

Macduff Both.

Don't worry.

McAlpin rises to speak.

McAlpin The Scots chiefs here know my position, I need not rehearse what we all already know so I will instead address my words to England.

The old tyrant is gone but his queen is still alive. This woman has the blood on her hands of countless of our people. This woman used every means at her disposal to dominate our country. We come here invited to a gathering and we find that not only is she alive, she is comfortably installed in Dunsinane under the protection of England.

I speak from Appin and Sutherland and Tain and the people of Angus and the Kingdom of Fife. We have come here to say – install Malcolm as king and we will accept him but there can be no peace in Scotland as long as the Queen remains in Dunsinane.

Macduff We thank you, McAlpin, for speaking on behalf of your people. You've spoken clearly and you've been heard. Now I call on Earl Moray to speak on behalf of his people.

Siward He doesn't leave much room for compromise.

Macduff There's plenty room.

Siward 'There can be no peace as long as the Queen remains in Dunsinane.'

It's unequivocal.

Macduff It all depends on the definition of the words.

Siward Which words?

Macduff 'Peace', 'Queen', 'remain' and 'Dunsinane'.

Moray Look at us. Here at the beck of an English commander. Is this Scotland now? Try to see us as our children will see us when they look back on this day in time to come. They would be humiliated. It should shame us to kneel before an invader, but it seems we have no shame left. We in Moray will never accept Malcolm as king. The royal line passes through the Queen to her son. Wherever he is – hiding in whichever cave or castle – the Queen's son is the rightful King and we'll defend him to the death.

Macduff Thank you, Moray. You have spoken clearly and you have been heard. The last speaker I call is Lord Siward to speak on behalf of England.

Siward Scotland has been at war for many years. On either side there are parties with wounds and each party wants their wounds avenged and each act of vengeance is punished with vengeance and so if you do nothing now the war will continue until there is nobody left alive in Scotland and all that exists is the mountains and the empty land and the grudge that hangs above it.

In the last months I've travelled to every part of the country and I've talked to you. I know that there are those who cannot accept the Queen's son as king. I know there are those who can never accept Malcolm as king.

So England proposes a marriage.

Let the Queen marry Malcolm.

Let the Queen's son be Malcolm's heir.

Let the two great houses of Scotland be united.

Macduff What does Malcolm say?

Malcolm I'm a little . . . taken aback.
But.
Impressed.

England, you are subtler than I thought.

McAlpin Would this arrangement be enforced by England?

Siward We would enforce it.

McAlpin Is this arrangement the preferred arrangement of England?

Siward It is.

Macduff What does the party of Moray say?

Moray Sister.
Did you know about this proposal?

Gruach [No.]

Moray [What should I say?]

Silence.

Macduff The proposal put before the Queen is clear. What do you say?

Gruach I accept.

Macduff Scotland is decided.

Let us prepare to celebrate a wedding.

Music is played.

Gruach leaves the hall.
Siward follows her.

Siward I had no choice.

Gruach Nor I – it seems.

Siward This way brings peace.

And now – at least – you are Queen again.

Gruach I was never not Queen.

Siward No.

Gruach You're ashamed.

Aren't you?

That makes it worse.

Siward This is the best way for Scotland.

And you know that.

You have accepted.

Haven't you?

Gruach I have accepted my fate.

Siward Good.

I wish it could have been different.

Gruach So do I.

A moment.

Siward The song they're singing.
What is it?

Gruach A wedding song.

Siward What does it say?

Gruach It calls out to the relatives of the bride.
It tells them there is a wedding.
It says she needs attendants.
It asks them to come.
In great number.

*

Gruach is prepared for a wedding.
The Great Hall is laid for a feast.

Gruach Boy –

Boy Soldier Yes, Ma'am.

Gruach Tell them I'm ready.

Boy Soldier Yes, Ma'am.

The Boy Soldier goes to leave.

Gruach Boy.

Boy Soldier Yes, Ma'am.

Gruach How do I look?

The Boy Soldier considers.

Boy Soldier Magical.

Gruach Good.

You're learning.

>   *The Hall.*
>   *Noblemen and women dance a formal dance.*
>   *Malcolm invites Gruach to dance.*
>   *She dances with him.*
>   *Siward watches.*
>   *The dance ends.*
>   *Applause.*

>   *The hall doors open.*

Egham Sir – there's a problem, Sir.

>   *Scottish Soldiers enter the hall, weapons raised.*
>   *They are covered in blood.*

Macduff Where are the guards?

Egham Dead, Sir.

Siward What do they want?

Gruach They are mine.

They have come for me.

>   *Gruach walks towards them and out of the hall.*

>   *The Scottish Soldiers attack the crowd.*

>   *The crowd defend themselves.*

>   *The hall is full of fire and slaughter.*

No one saw how the Queen's men entered Dunsinane.
The doors opened silently and afterwards we found that
All our sentries had been cut at the throat – but
However her men came the mysterious thing was her
    leaving,

How calmly she walked towards them – these blood-
    covered men –
And whether their coming came of witchcraft or of
    treachery
Or some combination of the two – as the great hall filled
    up
With fire and blood one thought filled the room like smoke.
She knew – she knew – she knew.

Siward puts on his armour.

Three

AUTUMN

An English force returns to Dunsinane.
  The Great Hall is now an encampment.
  A fire, some food, and a chance to rest.

The English bring with them a cart.
  On the cart, a body.

After we buried Tom and John the Cook and Henry
And Harry and Dan the Falconer we set out again
To fetch back the Queen and her son to Dunsinane.
For four weeks we ranged for them across the hills and,
Mother, you have not seen hills like these – never –
Unless you've been to either Hell or Scotland –
And I don't expect you've been to either place.

These hills rise up in great grey slabs at crazy angles
So steep the green just slides off of them – or else they stand
Like black ships on a sea of watery moor – or else some
  of them
Look like the backs of beasts, a bear say or a cow – a
  giant cow
Lying down – a sick cow, so it's twisted and lying down –
Not on a field of nice grass, no – but on a pile of more
Rolled and twisted beasts under it – a heap – a heap
  of beasts.

And the paths up these hills, Mother, they're as narrow
  and wet
As the scramble from beach to clifftop – only more
  narrow –
And more wet – and these cliffs rise a mile up and it's not
  beach below

88

But the black waters of one of these freezing lakes they
   have
That nothing lives in and on top of the hills nothing but
   snow –
Fields of frozen snow – and a cloud that never seems to
   lift.

But these are the places where our enemies hide and so
These are the places where we look for them – walking
   behind
Our commander who goes ahead of us always –
   marching on
Into the mist – the sound of his armour sometimes is all
   we hear
As we walk up into the dark glen. Not much to talk about
And no songs as these hills make a punishment of every
   day.

But Siward says we must insist on understanding this
   country
Even if its people insist on resisting us, so he finds high
   places
And he says, 'Down there and there and there and there
Is where they're likely hiding.' And so we go down there
   and there
To clear whatever cave or bothy he's found and smoke
   out who's in it
And if we meet a fight we set about it hard, Mother – and
   we always win.
We win because if we don't win – we lose – and if we lose –
Then what?

   The English return from the expedition.

   Egham enters.

Egham Morning, lads.

— Morning, Sir.

89

Egham sees the cart.

Egham Oh.
Dead?

— Yes, Sir.

Egham Who?

— Edward.

Egham Edward?

— Edward the archer, Sir.

Egham Fuck.
How?

— Cow trod on him.

— In the night, Sir.

— In Glen Lyon.

— We heard word that the Queen's son was hiding there.

— So Siward marched us.

— Overnight.

— Once we got there.

— We waited till it got dark and then.

— He says, 'Surround the village.'

— So we took positions in the woods and fields and wait.

— Silent.

— Edward took a position too.

— Lay down on the ground of a field.

— And waits.

— And in the night a cow.

— Trod on his leg.

— Must've broke it.

— A great big hairy cow.

— Crack.

— Edward didn't say anything.

— He didn't even make a noise.

— I was right next to him all night.

— Nothing.

— In the morning – Siward shouts and we attack –

— We surprise them.

— They're in their beds.

— We win.

— It's easy.

— Afterwards we gather all their men together.

— We gather all their women and children.

— There's all that sorting to be done.

— Siward walks up the line of them.

— 'Where's the Queen's son?'

— That's Siward.

— 'Which one of these boys is the Queen's son?'

— No one speaks.

— Silence.

— No matter how hard we make it for them.

— No one speaks.

— So Siward says if they won't tell us which boy it is – we'll take all the boys.

— So –

— Well –

— Well we've still got to sort the rest of them –

— It's hard work – it's a hard day –

— Fire and smoke.

— Anyway.

— It's long into the afternoon before we come to leaving and that's when we realise.

— No Edward.

— I found him.

— I found him.

— We both found him.

— A whole day he'd been lying there in the field.

— We put him on the back of the cart, but he was dead by yesterday.

— Poor Edward.

— He didn't say a word that whole night.

— If he'd made a noise they would have heard us.

— But he didn't make a sound.

— Not a sound.

Egham Must have hurt.

— Must have, Sir.

Egham Poor Edward.

— Yes, Sir.

Egham Take him up to the field and bury him.

— Yes, Sir.

— Shall we bring in the prisoners, Sir?

Egham Bring them in.

> *The English Soldiers lead in a small group of teenage boys.*
> *They boys are tied together in a chain so they can't escape.*

Egham Only boys.

— Siward said only take the boys.

Egham What did you do with the men?

— Burned them.

*

Siward's rooms.
> *Siward takes off his armour and his boots, and washes the soot off his face.*
> *The Boy Soldier attends to him.*

Egham You burned them?

Siward That's right.

Egham Alive?

Siward Yes.

Egham Right.

> . . .
> Burned them alive?

Siward Yes.

Egham Well.

Siward What?

Egham It's just it's –

Siward What?

Egham It's –

Siward What?

Egham It's a bit Scandinavian, isn't it?

Siward Every man had a chance to speak.
One of those boys is the Queen's son.
If even one of those men had spoken
They could all be alive now.

Egham I can understand threatening people or bullying or torturing even – you expect to have to do that because those are reasonable – effective even – ways to glean – because one wants information – but to burn people alive?

That makes them dead.

Siward If we make a threat we have to follow it through.

Egham You could have brought them back to Dunsinane. At least there's a value in hostages. There's no value in corpses.

Siward This is not a war in pursuit of wealth, Egham.

Egham What is it in pursuit of then?

Siward Peace.

Egham Well, do we have to be quite so ruthless in the pursuit of peace?

Siward Every day one or other of our boys comes back to us laid out on a cart and marked with wounds which come from *her* arrows – cuts which come from *her* knives. She is ruthless. So we have to be ruthless.

Egham They're not fighting us because of their Queen. They're fighting us because we're here. The Scots will fight anyone who's standing in front of them. They like fighting. In fact – they're fighting us partly because we're stopping them from fighting each other.

Siward English or Scottish – people cluster behind the side they think is the stronger. They must believe we are the stronger.

Egham Do you think burning them helps?

Siward It shows we're determined.

Egham Determined to do what?

Siward Determined to win.

Egham This war belongs to Malcolm and Macduff. Let them do what's best to secure the country for themselves and let's leave a garrison on the Forth to protect Northumbria and let's you and I go back to England – let's let you go back to your rivers and moors and farms and let me go back to Surrey where it's warm and I've got fields and a wife.

Siward You sound like you would prefer us to be defeated.

Egham Who said 'defeated'? I didn't say 'defeated'. Did you say 'defeated'? I didn't say 'defeated'. I said 'leave'.

Siward 'Defeated' – 'leave' – what's the difference?

Egham All the difference.

Siward We will leave when we win.

Egham Winning isn't a fact, Siward – winning is a decision we take.

Siward Egham – look out there.
   The Queen is free.
   She is killing our men every day.
   In ambush, massacre and trick.
   Does that look like winning to you?

Egham I could be persuaded.

Siward One of those boys is hers.

   Find him.

*

The castle yard.

The Hen Girl enters.
   Soldiers notice.

The Hen Girl walks along the line of prisoners and gives them some bread and some water.

The Hen Girl continues down the line in silence.

The Soldiers watch.

— Which one do you think it is?

— The one with the eyes.

— They've all got eyes.

— The one with the eyes that look right at you.

— Why?

— Look at the way he's looking at us.
   Full of –

— Contempt?

— No –

— Pity?

— No –

— What?

— As though we're very far away from him.
Very small.

— Oh.

— Might just be bad eyesight.

— Looks don't mean anything. You could take a girl –
take any girl – take the hen girl for example –

— Just for example –

— Put her in a blue gown – dress the hen girl in a royal-
blue gown then see how she'd look at us –

— Still wouldn't make her a princess.

— Would make her look like a princess.

— She looks like a princess now.

— I can just see her – walking across the hall floor in the
light of a fire –

— Who?

— The hen girl.
Walking across the hall floor in her blue gown.
Beautiful.

— Too beautiful for you.

— Soft hands.

— The hen girl?

— The Queen's son.

— Not necessarily.

— I think we'd know him because he'd have the sort of
soft hands you get if you've spent your life touching

leather and swan and horses and butter and things of that type.

— I don't think so.

— Soft things.

— This Queen's son's been a long time away from butter.

— This Queen's son's been out in the woods.

— He's been riding and fighting.

— This Queen's son's hands would be the same as yours or mine – hard.

— Silken hair.

— Silken hair?

— Silken hair.

— What are you talking about?

— We will know him by his silken hair.

— Why?

— That's what songs say.

— Songs?

— 'There came a noble prince with silken hair.'

— Which song is that?

— I don't know exactly but –

— Sing it –

— No. I'm not saying it *is* a song, I'm saying that it's *like* a song.

— (*Sings.*) 'There came a noble prince with silken hair.'

— Stop it.

— 'And I did bum his bottom bare.'

— I just said –

— 'And I did stroke his pubic hair.'

— All right.
  That's enough.

— 'Of hairy balls he had a pair.'

— Enough!

— I'm only saying –

— Princesses have silken hair.
  Maidens have silken hair.
  Ladies fair have silken hair.
  Not princes.
  Princes are bold, handsome and cruel.

— Then it's none of these boys.
  No bold handsome cruel princes here.
  These princes are small – small, spotty and afraid.

— I still think it's the one with the eyes.

One Prisoner talks to the Hen Girl as she feeds him.

Prisoner [Thank you. You're kind.]

Hen Girl [I will bring you more food if I can.]

Prisoner [What will they do to us?]

Hen Girl [I can't speak to you.
  They'll hit me for speaking.]

— Quiet!

— Oi!

— No speaking.

A Soldier hits the Prisoner who spoke.
  He raises a hand to strike the Hen Girl.

— Don't.

The Soldier doesn't hit the Hen Girl.
The Hen Girl smiles at the Soldier who spoke.
He smiles back.

— Look at her.
In that blue gown.
Walking across the floor of the hall,
Silken hair.
Look at her.
Princess.

Egham enters.
He looks at the prisoners.

Which one do you want to talk to first, Sir?

Egham This one.

— Which one?

Egham The one with the eyes.

A Prisoner is chosen.

Strip him.

. . .
DO IT.

The Soldiers begin to strip the boy.
The boy resists. He shouts – fights.
He is afraid.
The boy is subdued.

Egham looks at the boy.

It's not him.
Scars on his back from a whipping.
Nobody whips princes.

Egham looks down the line again.

This one.

The next boy is stripped.
    He resists.
    He is angry.

Egham studies this boy.

Skin and bones.
    Never a prince that badly fed.

    . . .
    This one.

The next boy is stripped.
    The one with the eyes.
    He is calm.

Egham inspects the third boy.

The Soldier turns the boy round.

— Sir –

Egham What?

On his ankle, Sir.

Egham looks.
    A tattoo.

Egham Three snakes devouring a moon.

    . . .
    His skin's unbroken.
    What sort of boy reaches fifteen and has unbroken
skin?
    What sort of boy hasn't even ever fallen out of a tree?
    Untie him.

The Soldiers separate the boy from the others.

Look at you.
    A bundle of bones and breath and not much else.
    It seems cold to kill you.
    I know you can't understand my words

But maybe you can hear it in my voice.
I'm sorry.
But I really really want to go home.
. . .
Take him to Siward.

— What shall we do with the rest of them, Sir?

Egham Put them on a cart.
Take them to Perth.
Sell them as slaves to the Danes there.
Divide what gold you get between you all.
That's your reward.
Go.

— Sir.

Egham What?

— Sir . . . this one's got a tattoo as well.

Egham What?

Egham looks. Another boy, another tattoo.

— Sir . . . this one does too.

— Sir . . . and this one.

— Sir . . . I think they might all have tattoos, Sir.

Egham FUCK!
FUCK!

Egham hits the boy he chose.

Which one of you is the King?
Which one of you is the fucking King?

The boy cringes beneath the blows.

*

The Great Hall.
  Malcolm entertains two Scottish chiefs with drink and food.
  A girl sings a Gaelic song, maybe she plays the harp.

Siward enters.

Malcolm Siward, you're back.

Siward You called for me.

Malcolm Come and join us.

Siward I was expecting a private audience.

Malcolm But we have visitors.
  The Chiefs of Kintyre and Luss,
  And they've come all this way.
  Isn't she beautiful?
  She's from Ireland.
  Luss brought her.
  He knows my tastes.
  Have a drink.

Siward I'll return when you're less busy.

Malcolm dismisses the singer.

Malcolm Here – take some wine.
  Go to my bed and prepare another song.
  Something about love.
  Make sure it's got plenty of verses.

He introduces the two Chiefs.

Luss – Kintyre – this is our commander, Siward.

Luss We've waited to meet you.

Kintyre And here you are.

Luss But now you're here.

Kintyre We're ashamed.

Luss We don't have a gift for you.

Siward I don't expect to receive gifts.

Luss No.

Kintyre We heard that.

Luss You receive no gifts.

Kintyre But we do expect to give them.

Luss It's our custom.

Kintyre It's a matter of honour.

Luss We have to bring you something.

Kintyre Gold. Or meat. Or a woman.

Luss Even if you don't want the gift given.

Kintyre But we don't know what you like.

Siward It's not important.

Luss All this time you've been here and still we don't know.

Kintyre You English.

Luss You keep your desires a secret.

Kintyre Malcolm likes women.

Luss What does England like?

Kintyre What gift can we give England?

Luss Can we ask you now?

Kintyre Now that you're here.

Luss Can we ask?

Kintyre Do you mind?

Luss Now that you're here in Scotland.

Kintyre Can we ask?

Both What do you want?

Siward Peace.

Kintyre Mmm.

Luss Well.

Kintyre Peace.

Luss You're sure you don't want a girl?

Kintyre Or a boy?

Luss Only peace.

Kintyre That's a difficult gift.

Luss We don't have it to give.

Kintyre We used to have peace but . . .

Luss Not now.

Kintyre Not any more.

Luss Still – if we didn't bring peace.

Kintyre Maybe we can leave it – by going.

Luss Leave you in peace – he means.

Kintyre It's a play on the words.

Siward I understood.

Kintyre Let that be our gift then.

Luss We give you the gift of our going.

Siward I accept.

Thank you.

> *Luss and Kintyre leave.*

Siward I didn't want to end your party.

Malcolm But nevertheless you did.

Siward I apologise.

Malcolm The chiefs told me that you've been off travelling again.

Siward Yes.

Malcolm Crossing the country in pursuit of the Queen.

Siward I made some progress this time.

Malcolm They say you show no mercy.

Siward I will cut off the rebellion at its head.

Malcolm It's a very astute strategy.

At least it would have been when she was in our custody.

Siward This time we made a breakthrough.

Malcolm Mmm.

Siward Egham heard the Queen's son was hiding in Glen Lyon. I swept the valley and collected every boy of the right age.

Egham is conducting interrogations now.

We'll find him.

Malcolm It really seems the war is progressing – strongly.

Siward I hope so.

Malcolm Good.

Siward Yes.

Malcolm Only I wonder if it isn't progressing *too* strongly.

Siward What?

Malcolm Talking to the chiefs.
  You know how they talk.
  Grievance after grievance.
  I drift.
  And I found myself wondering
  If things aren't going *too* well.

Siward How is that possible?

Malcolm Siward – my chiefs don't offer me fealty out of
moral concern or even love –

Siward They offer you fealty because you are the rightful
king.

Malcolm Wouldn't that be good if they did?
  But no.
  They offer me fealty because I am weak. I don't
threaten them. The stronger I am, the more they begin to
wonder if one day I might be strong enough to – overpower
them. They start wondering if it isn't in their interest to
balance my power by supporting the Queen.

Siward The Chief in Glen Lyon was on the Queen's side.

Now he knows that was not in his interest.

Malcolm In so far as he's dead. Yes.

I would have preferred you to show restraint.

Siward You don't restrain a dog when he's chasing a deer.

Not if you want to get fed.

Malcolm Glen Lyon was not a dangerous man, Siward,
he was a coward. He was quietly waiting to see which
way this war went. Now that you've killed him – his
relatives have been forced to decide which side they're
on. It seems now they've joined the Queen.

Siward Then I will send a troop up that valley again and
I will burn it again.

Malcolm Why on earth would you want to do that?

Siward To draw a line.

Malcolm Stop.

Siward What?

Malcolm Just –
Siward, please.
You must stop.
Stop this.
This incessant
Definition.

There are patterns of loyalty between us – there are
alliances – there are friends who say they're friends but
work against us and others who say they're enemies but
quietly help us – there are networks of obligation between
us – there are marriages and births between us – there are
narrowly balanced feuds between us – feuds that only
need the smallest breath of the wrong word spoken to tip
them into war –

There are patterns between us.

And into that very delicate filigree you are putting your
fist.

Siward I'm a soldier. I like clarity.

Malcolm Clarity is dangerously close to crudity.

Siward And subtlety is dangerously close to corruption.

Malcolm Be aware that I am listening to the words you
choose very carefully.

Siward Good.

Then listen to this.

You disgust me.

Wine.
    Ease.
    Song.
    Silk.

While out there my boys are dying on your behalf.

You are corrupt, Malcolm.

Depthless.

Weak.

You wallow in your own venality.

It seems.

Malcolm Mmm.

. . .

Do you ever ask yourself, Siward, if it's possible that I might in fact want to create the appearance of wallowing in venality?

. . .

Does that thought ever occur to you?

. . .

Or is that thought too subtle – too corrupt – a bird for your wooden English hands to catch?

. . .

They bring me wine – the chiefs – they bring me women – they think – I'm corrupt – I'm weak – I wallow in venality – they think – this King is easy – he won't cause trouble for us – all he wants is to be left alone to enjoy his wine and his women – let him be King – better him than someone other – better him than someone strong – someone with more – definition.

Let Malcolm stay – at least until someone better comes along . . .

. . .

But no one better will ever come along.

And do you want to know why?
Because they'll all kill each other before they kill me.
. . .
My weakness is my strength.

Siward That might be a plausible strategy, Malcolm, were it not for the fact that you actually *do* want to be left alone to enjoy your wine and your women – you actually *are* weak. It's not an appearance – it's true.

Malcolm The best way to maintain the appearance of something being true is for it to actually be true.

Siward This is all words, Malcolm. What do you want me to do? Give up?

Malcolm I don't want you to stop your enthusiastic pursuit of the Queen, Siward.

I'm just asking you to accomplish it by more nuanced means.

Siward I'm sorry. I don't know what 'nuanced means' means.

Malcolm Withdraw your men to Dunsinane for the winter. Let your soldiers recover. Let me be weak for a while. Let the Queen start to make mistakes. If the chiefs think she might win they'll soon start to plot against her. We can execute some little raids, assassinations. Let them spend winter in a world of uncertainty.

Then when spring comes – see how they'll welcome us back.

Siward What about our allies?

Malcolm Give them money.

That's what I was discussing with Luss and Kintyre just now.

Siward A chief should pay tribute to the King. It isn't the other way around.

Malcolm You madden me, Siward.

You must take gifts from the chiefs.

A king repays a gift tenfold.

By taking nothing you offer nothing.

Siward I know the game.

It's corrupt.

I ignored it.

Malcolm Siward, your insistence on governing by force is making being king very difficult for me.

Siward If you find being king becoming tiresome there are chiefs who could take the position from you.

Malcolm Sometimes I find being alive becoming tiresome. Do you know anyone who can take that position from me?

Siward You're drunk.

Malcolm Join me.

Malcolm offers wine to Siward.

Siward Maybe you'd prefer to go back to England?

Malcolm Lovely England.

No.

But maybe you would like to go back.

Siward Why?

Malcolm I don't know.

You just seem tired.

Siward, you lost a son in Scotland. Be careful you don't lose your mind here as well.

Siward I am still commander.

Malcolm And I am still King.

Siward No.

You are not a king, Malcolm. You're not a king in Scotland. You're not a king in Dunsinane. You're not even a king in this room.

Kings rule.

When you talk about kingship you talk about who's friends with who and who said what and what things mean and what gifts to give . . .

You make the problems of being a king sound like the problems of being a woman.

You're right, I'm tired, Malcolm. I'm tired of 'appear' and I'm tired of 'seem'. I only have bone and flesh and mud and bog and metal. That's the world my power's in and that's the world I'll fight in, and that's the world in which I'll win.

Malcolm Mmm.

Siward I'll win.

*

Night
> *The castle yard.*
> *A fire.*
> *The English Soldiers sing.*
> *Their song cheers them up.*

— Whisky.

— Whisky.

— Whisky.

— Where'd it come from?

— Egham.

— Good old Egham.

— To Egham!

— Where did Egham get it?

— Two Scots lords came to see the King and the cook said to me it was one Scots lord who brought a whisky barrel with him.

— And Egham stole it?

— No, Egham bought it.

— What did he buy it with?

— Something.

— There's always something with Egham.

— He's clever.

— He's always got a finger up someone's arse has Egham.

— No matter where he is he finds someone who's got something he wants.

— And he gets it.

— Put Egham in the middle of a field of snow.

— On top of these hills.

— And he'd still find someone.

— He'd build a snowman.

— He'd give it a little pair of frosty balls.

— And then he'd tickle them.

— And that snowman would give him water.

— To Egham!

— Cold though.

— Cold.

— Winter coming.

— What shall we fire at?

— George's shoe.

— All right. George's shoe.

— What do you get if you hit George's shoe?

— Whoever hits George's shoe gets off with the hen girl tonight.

The first Archer fires an arrow at a shoe.
It misses.

— Bollocks.

— Edward would have hit that.

— Edward would have hit it and he would have got off with the hen girl.

— With Edward gone at least you've got a chance.

— I'd prefer it if Edward were here.

The third Archer fires.
Misses.

— I'm bored of this.

— Doesn't help that it's cold.

— Whisky, though.

— Whisky doesn't help either.